I0606101

DIANA LOUG

EMBROIDERED KNITS

OVER 25 **MOTIFS**
TO PERSONALIZE AND EMBELLISH
YOUR OWN KNITWEAR

CONTENTS

EMBROIDERY DESIGNS

JOIN ME ON MY EMBROIDERY JOURNEY

'When did you start embroidering?' is a question that I'm often asked. It's difficult to pin down exactly when I started, as I grew up with all sorts of handicrafts around me, and it's always been a part of my life: my paternal grandmother taught me to knit, crochet and embroider when I was too little to remember, and my mother made clothes and knitted matching outfits for me and my two sisters; she also often mended damaged clothes with embroidery or a patch.

It isn't very easy to explain why I started embroidering, but I know that it was partly down to the realization that embroidery can have many different functions, and is a great way to create interesting clothes. It can be used to decorate a garment and give it a unique, personal look. You can transform old clothes and give them a new lease of life. If you choose thread colours that go well with the other clothes you're wearing, embroidery on a garment can help tie a whole outfit together. And, last but not least, you can embroider over spots or holes to make damaged garments wearable again; depending on the size of the hole and the design chosen, you may need to back the hole and design with cut-away stabilizer to add some security.

So if you haven't embroidered before – why not? Embroidery is for everyone, and embroidery on knitting is something that can give pleasure regardless of age. It's also very easy to create your own style with embroidery, and stitch something you'll love for years to come. If you need a helping hand with embroidery stitches, there's an embroidery techniques section at the beginning of this book that takes you step by step through my favourite stitches, alongside helpful photographs.

Only 11 stitches are needed to make all 25 designs in this book, showing you how versatile and experimental you can be with just a few techniques. I have designed lots of embroidery motifs to transform your knitted pieces into wonderful works of art. I've focused mainly on garments, but there's no reason why you couldn't embroider on a knitted bag, sofa pillow covers, and other homewares and accessories. Don't be afraid to mix and match different embroidery motifs too, for results that are truly unique.

I hope you will join me on this embroidery journey. Good luck with embroidering, and if you fancy sharing what you make online, please add the hashtag #lougknitwear; that would be extra nice.

Diana Loug

CHOOSING EMBROIDERY MOTIFS AND A COLOUR PALETTE

The sort of embroidery I choose is usually determined by the type of knit I am dealing with. I always start by studying the shape, lines and structure of the knitted piece so I can adapt the design of the embroidery to suit it. Below are some of the things I consider:

- Does the knit have soft curves, or does it have straight lines and a slightly more angular shape?
- Is the knitting made of chunky or delicate yarn?
- Are the stitches large or small?
- What colour is the knitting? A neutral colour is like a blank canvas, and allows me to be more creative with my embroidery-colour selection; however, a colourful knitted background may require more consideration. If it is a subdued colour, often I choose to work the embroidery in a single colour that is similar in shade to the knitted piece, or a colour from the neighbouring colours in the colour wheel (take a look at Itten's 12-hue colour wheel for more information). If the knit is a strong colour, I choose to embroider in colours that are equally bold.
- Would it work well if I were to choose a motif that features many different shades of colour, based on the colour of the knit? A neutral-coloured knitted piece allows for a larger palette, but a colourful knit may mean I need to limit my colours.

The next thing I plan is the look I want to create. Should the embroidery be muted and delicately charming, or do I want it to be sizeable and showy? It's after this that I decide on the colours I want to use. If I'm still not sure about the overall impression, I make a sketch of the knitted piece then draw the embroidery design on it. If I like the look of it, I'm ready to embroider. At other times, my only starting point is the colours I've decided on, and then the embroidery takes shape as I go along. This is a much more organic process, but I enjoy not knowing how the design will end up.

When you're going to embroider on knitting, you need to think about the density of the stitches when choosing motifs. Items knitted on thinner needles give you a denser layer to embroider on than those knitted on thicker needles. Motifs with small details don't work well when you're embroidering over large knitting stitches: you will notice that you don't have a firm base on which to embroider, as the gaps between the stitches will be too big.

In this book, the embroidery motifs are adapted to the various garments. They are chosen on the basis of the density of the stitches and the design of the garment. Bear in mind that when embroidering a large design it is important not to place your stitches too close together, as this will make the knitting less stretchy under the embroidery and may result in a bumpy, distorted appearance.

Embroidering may perhaps seem a bit challenging, but it isn't so difficult. If you are a knitter, you will probably have the equipment you need at hand, and you'll find most of the embroideries in this book are worked with knitting yarns. My tip is to practise on a sample, such as a knitted swatch, and play around with different stitches. The embroidery stitches won't be uniform when worked on knitting, but don't forget that this is part of what makes the embroidery unique. If the process is new to you, start with the simplest motifs, such as a single flower; that's the easiest way to get a good result – and feel a sense of achievement. The bigger the embroidery, the greater the degree of difficulty will be.

CHOOSING YOUR YARN AND NEEDLES, AND THE SEARCH FOR INSPIRATION

For the embroidery patterns you will need only small amounts of yarn in one or more colours. This is a great way to use up left-over yarn you may have. If you haven't got particular shades, maybe you know someone else who knits or crochets, and you can swap yarn with them. You can use the brands and colours I've chosen for the motifs, or select your own favourite colours from your existing stash. If you opt to choose your own, and the embroidered knit is for you, pick colours that make you feel happy, and you are comfortable with.

If you think putting colours together is difficult, you are not alone in this. As a starting point, look at things you find beautiful, and use their colours to help you make your yarn choices. Begin by looking at the landscape around you for inspiration. For example, I live in a seaside town in south-west Norway, and it has stunning scenery: from the sea and beach to the rocks and vegetation, there are so many wonderful, harmonious colour combinations to be seen. It has influenced several of my embroidery motifs in this book, as well as the photographs. Also, take a look at the textiles and artworks you surround yourself with, or take notice of in books, magazines and furniture: I love to collect pieces of old fabric, for instance, as often I'm drawn to their attractive colours and shapes.

If a particular colour combination doesn't sing to me in an embroidery I'm working on, I will keep a note of it to use for future designs.

A lot can also be said for simply doodling with paints and colouring pencils when you're struggling to think of colourways; sometimes, just playing with shades with no design in mind can lead to exciting discoveries.

Maybe you're wondering what kind of needle you should choose. Bear in mind that choosing exactly the right needle will make embroidering much easier. You will need a long, thin, sharp yarn needle for almost all types of stitches, except for duplicate stitch (see page 16) and weaving (see page 17); for these techniques, you should use a blunt yarn needle.

EMBROIDERY SCHOOL

Here are the stitches I've used for all the embroideries in this book. If you are embroidering on knitting for the first time, I recommend you practise on a knitted swatch to start with. To fasten off, sew to and fro a few times at the back of the work.

I have suggested yarns and colours to embroider with throughout the book; however, feel free to use yarns and colours you have in your own stash.

Take care to leave enough space between your embroidery stitches. If they are too close together, your knit will pucker.

For beginners, I recommend placing your knitting in an embroidery frame while you stitch, to keep its fabric taut and prevent any puckering or distortion.

TRANSFERRING DESIGNS

Having some kind of outline or marking on the knit before embroidering makes it easier to ensure a correct, balanced design and to fill in details later. Throughout the book, there are diagrams of the embroideries for you to scan and/or trace off and use.

There are different ways to trace, transfer and mark the embroidery designs onto the knitting, to start off the embroidery. Use one or a combination, depending on the design and your preference.

- Trace the design onto water-soluble paper, pin it to the knitting then stitch the design directly over the paper. Once the embroidery is complete, simply wash away the paper. **Important note:** I do not recommend this method if you are using thick yarns.
- Trace the outline only onto parchment / baking paper, then cut it out to make a template. Pin the template to the knitting, then draw around it with a fabric pen or tack / baste around it with waste yarn or embroidery thread. Remove the template then stitch.
- Either by tacking / basting or by drawing with a water-erasable fabric pen, create an outline freehand with the help of a reference diagram. Water-erasable pens work better on lighter-coloured knitting, and the tacking / basting method is ideal for very dark-coloured knits.
- Simply mark out the placement of the different elements with different-coloured stitch markers, then embroider freehand.

STEM STITCH

This is a 'line' stitch with a slightly twisted appearance. Stitches can be worked in a straight line or along a curve, and each stitch overlaps the previous one by half its length.

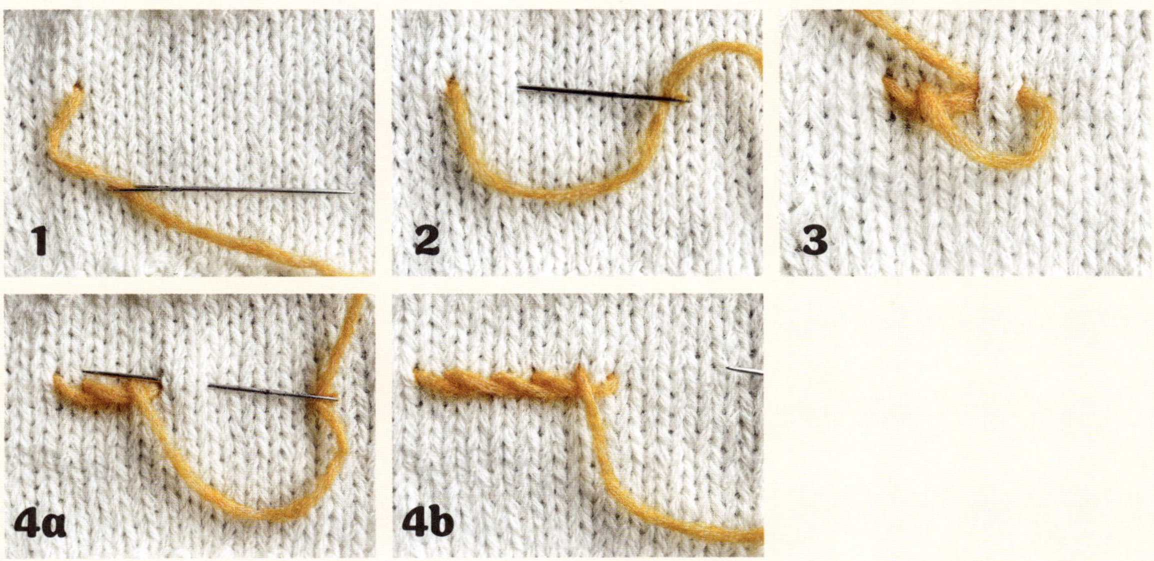

1. Bring the needle up from the wrong side of the work.
2. Take the needle back down into the kniting at the desired length, adding a little extra length to accommodate the overlap.
3. Bring the needle back and up again about halfway along the previous stitch.
4. Repeat steps 2 and 3 for every stitch, always keeping the working yarn to the same side of the needle.

BACKSTITCH

This produces an unbroken line of stitching. Every new stitch starts one stitch length beyond the previous one. Backstitch may be worked vertically, horizontally and diagonally.

1. Bring the needle up from the wrong side of the work (A).
2. Take it back down into the knitting, the desired stitch length away (B).
3. Bring the needle up ahead of the stitch just worked, the same distance away as the length of the previous stitch (C).
4. Insert the needle back down where the previous stitch ended (D).
5. Repeat steps 3 and 4 for every stitch.

SATIN STITCH

Satin stitch consists of parallel straight stitches lying close to one another, and is often used to fill and cover a shape. Some of the designs in the book feature vertical satin stitches; these are worked in the same way as detailed below, but with the stitches running vertically rather than horizontally.

1. To start, mark your desired outline onto the knitting to use as a guide. Having an outline of the motif to be embroidered makes it easier to fill in the details, and will give you a neater finish too.
2. Bring the needle up from the wrong side of the work, at one end of the shape and just on the outside of the outline. Take the needle down on the opposite side of the shape, again just on the outside of your outline, then back up on the first side. Continue to sew parallel stitches across the shape in the same way, gradually working towards the other end. The stitches should be close together, but in my experience they sit more neatly if there is a tiny distance between them – if they are too close, this can make the embroidery lumpy and too firm, making the knitting less stretchy.
3. Finish by taking the needle through to the wrong side and fastening off the end.

CHAIN STITCH

This stitch creates a line of small loops that look like the links of a chain. It's ideal for creating a decorative row of stitching, or for filling an area.

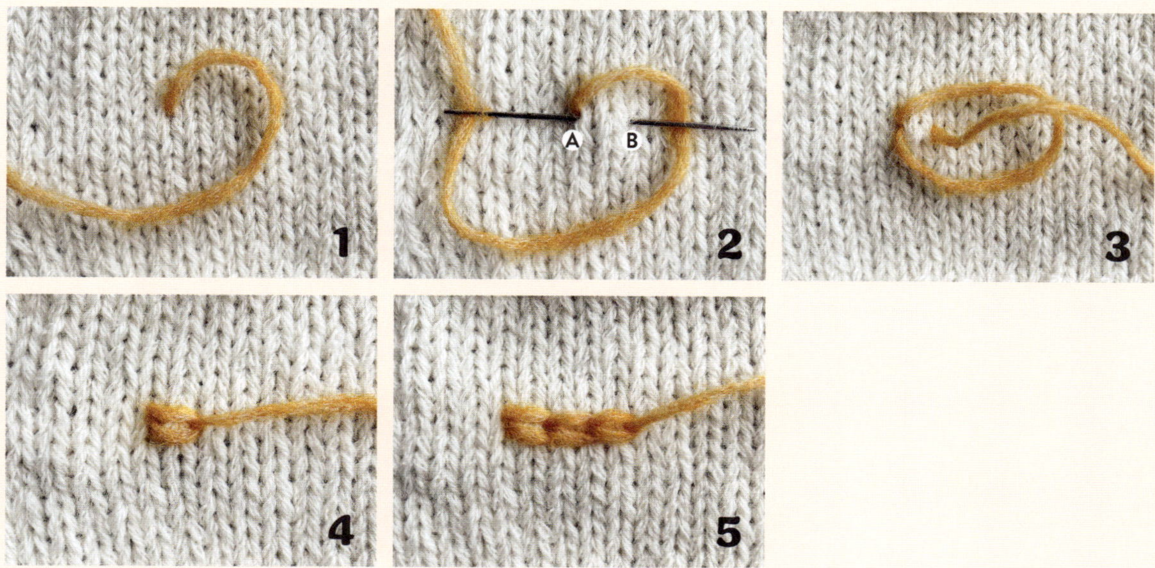

1. Bring the needle up from the wrong side of the work.
2. Take the needle down at A then out at B, without pulling the thread through. Arrange the working thread in a loop shape under the point of the needle.
3. Bring the needle out.
4. Tighten the thread gently, until you have a small loop.
5. Repeat steps 2–4 as desired. Finish the chain by securing the last loop: after step 4, take the needle down just on the outer side of the loop and then pull the thread gently through to the wrong side in the same way as for lazy daisy (detached chain) stitch (see page 14, step 2).

LAZY DAISY (DETACHED CHAIN) STITCH

Lazy daisy is almost the same as chain stitch, but the stitches are worked singly instead of in a continuous chain. As suggested by the name, this stitch is ideal for creating petal-like shapes for flower motifs.

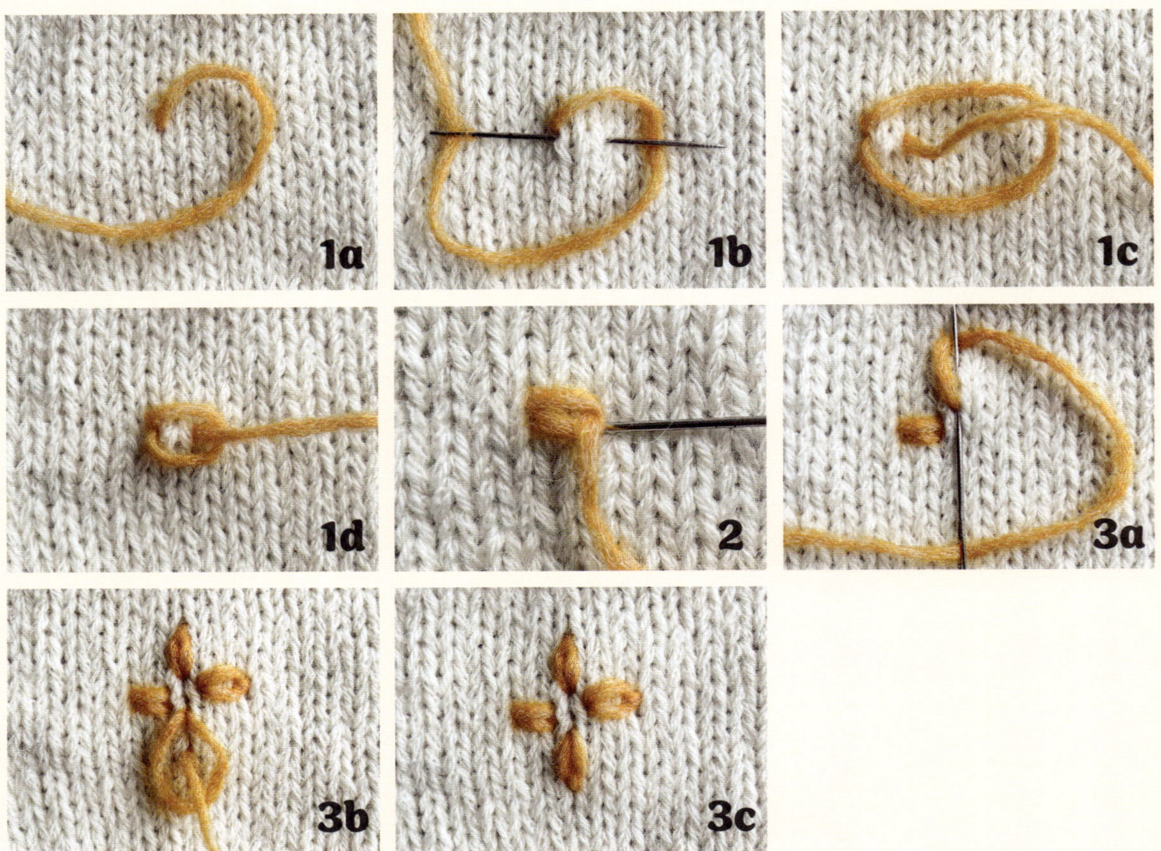

1. Work the first stitch as per steps 1–4 of chain stitch on page 13.
2. Complete the chain by securing the loop: after step 4, take the needle down just on the outer side of the loop and then pull the thread gently through to the back.
3. If you are going to embroider a whole flower, bring the needle up in the same place as for the first stitch, then take a stitch in the direction of your next petal and wrap the thread under the needle.

FRENCH KNOT

This decorative stitch is used for tiny circular details in motifs, such as little flower centres, and involves winding loops of thread round the needle.

1. Bring the needle up from the wrong side of the work at the point where you want the knot.
2. Wrap the thread two to four times round the tip of the needle. The number of times you wind it round will determine the size of the knot.
3. Position the tip of the needle close to your starting point. Holding the thread tight against the front of the work with your left index finger, push the loops down the needle until they touch the knitted surface.
4. Holding the loops in place with the tip of a finger or thumb, push the needle to the back of the work, pulling the thread through the loops.
5. Completed French knot. Repeat as many times as desired. To finish, take the needle to the back of the work and fasten off the end.

DUPLICATE STITCH

With this technique, you are embroidering a new stitch over a stitch of the knitted piece, and creating the appearance of a knit stitch. Note that you will need to use a blunt needle for duplicate stitch, known as a tapestry, darning or yarn needle; this prevents you from snagging and damaging the knitting.

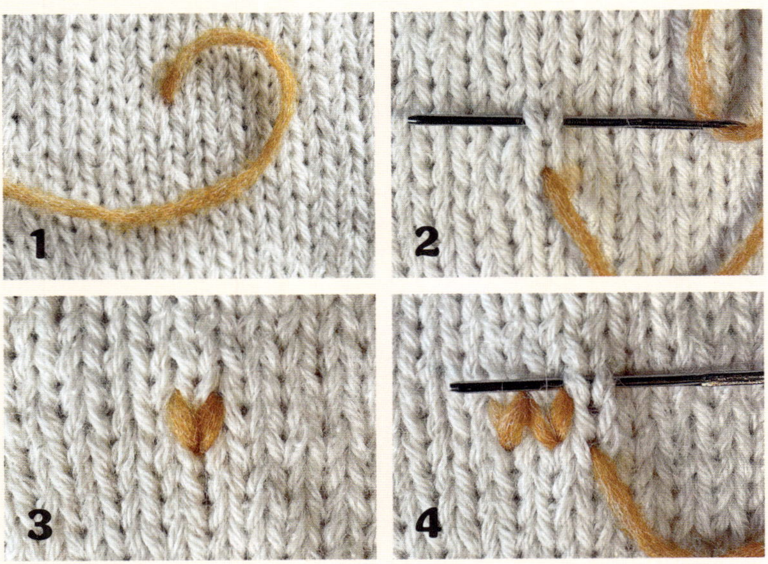

1. Bring the needle up from the wrong side of the work at the bottom of the 'V' of the knit stitch you want to cover.
2. Insert the needle behind the two 'legs' of the stitch above the one you wish to embroider, then pull the thread through to the front. The right-hand leg should now be covered.
3. To cover the left-hand leg and finish the stitch, insert the needle where you first brought it up, at the bottom of the 'V' of the stitch.
4. Repeat steps 1–3 to make as many duplicate stitches as desired. If you are embroidering a row of duplicate stitches, check that you are covering stitches from the same row or round.

WEAVING

This is the technique of weaving the needle over and under threads that lie across the direction in which you are weaving. It can be used to add a 3D effect to the embroidery, and is sometimes known as needle weaving. Use a blunt needle for the weaving, and an additional long needle – such as an extra-long tapestry needle or a double-pointed knitting needle – to wind your foundation threads around.

1. Position the long needle in the work by inserting it from the right side and bringing it up again a little way ahead.
2. Bring the needle with the embroidery thread up from the wrong side of the work, to the left of where the tip of the long needle came out. Bring the thread up and round the top of the needle.
3. Loop the thread around the other end of the needle, as shown.
4. Wrap the needle around the top and bottom of the needle once more. You should now have two threads on each side of the long needle.
5. You can now begin to weave over and under the four threads. Starting at the top and working from left to right, take the needle under thread 1, over thread 2, under thread 3 and over thread 4. Pull the thread tight, then use the weaving needle to push the thread you have just woven up to the top of the long needle. Now weave back, working from right to left: take the needle under thread 4, over thread 3, under thread 2 and over thread 1. Pull the thread through and gently tighten as before. Repeat until you reach the other end of the four threads held on the long needle. Use the working needle to gently press together the threads you have woven, and check that there is no space for more rows of weaving.
6. The completed weaving. Pull out the long needle holding the woven threads. Finish by sewing a few stitches at the end of the embroidery so it is firmly fixed to the layer below. Take the needle with the embroidery thread through to the wrong side of the work and fasten off the loose end.

CAST-ON STITCH

This is a raised, 3D stitch that's created by wrapping loops around the needle, pulling the thread through them then anchoring the stitch to the fabric. I like to use these when embroidering flowers.

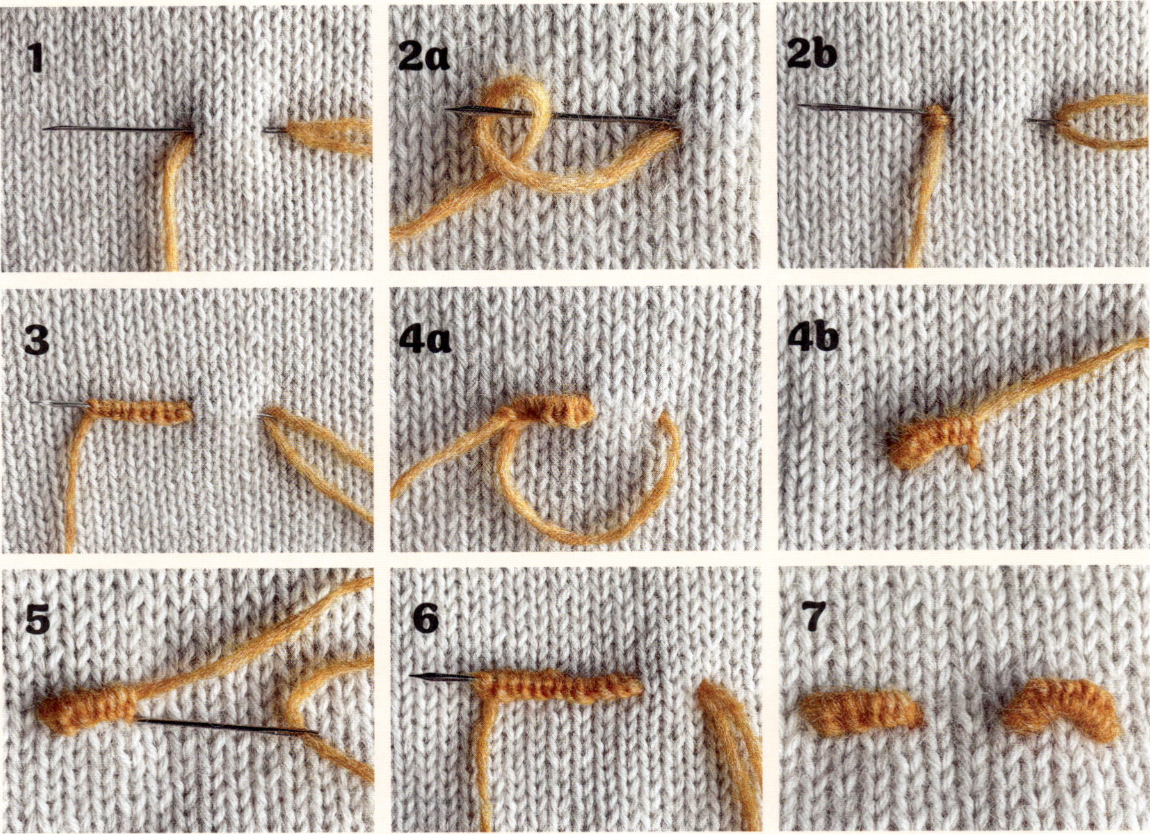

1. Bring the needle up from the wrong side of the work. Take it back down a little way from where you brought it up then up again at the original starting point. Don't pull the needle all the way through the work; stop where the eye is still visible, as shown.
2. Wrap the thread around the needle clockwise then under the working thread. Pull it tight.
3. Cast on more loops, as in step 2, until you have the desired length of stitches.
4. Now pull the needle and thread gently through all the loops until they lie flat on the work.
5. Fasten the stitch in place by inserting the needle at the end of the stitch.
6. If you want your stitch to form a curve, cast on loops until you have a slightly longer length than you want for your stitch; then follow steps 4 and 5 to secure the stitch on the fabric, and fasten off the end.
7. Straight cast-on stitch is shown on the left; curved cast-on stitch is shown on the right.

Feels Like Summer

Create a lush garland of flowers on your knitting. The design consists of flowers of various sizes, with pretty little leaves and other details in between. You could easily pick out one or two flowers to create your own motif. On the sample opposite, the embroidery spreads over the front and onto the shoulders of the sweater.

Embroidery techniques

- Satin stitch
- Chain stitch
- Lazy daisy (detached chain) stitch
- Cast-on stitch
- Straight stitch

Notions

- Long, thin, sharp yarn needle
- Scissors
- Stitch markers
- Embroidery frame (optional, but it can be very helpful to give you a taut and stable surface to embroider on, making it easier to avoid pulling the embroidery thread too tight)
- Water-soluble paper

Yarn

Sandnes Garn: Tynn Silk Mohair (57% mohair, 28% silk, 15% wool; 2-ply / lace / weight 0; 25g / 212m / 232yd)

10–15g Lime Punch 9523 (pale yellow-green)

10–15g Light Copper Brown 3535 (rust)

25g Powder Pink 3511 (blush pink)

10–15g Lemon 9004 (ice yellow)

10–15g Deep Burgundy 4372 (burgundy)

10–15g Light Acorn 3041 (warm taupe)

10–15g Jelly Bean Green 8236 (bright green)

Sandnes Garn: Alpakka Silke (70% alpaca, 30% mulberry silk; 4-ply / fingering / weight 1; 50g / 200m / 218yd)

50g Plum Pink 4043 (dark pink)

1

2

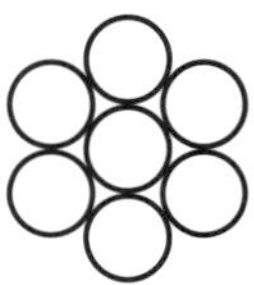

3

4

5

6

7

EMBROIDERY MOTIFS
(shown at actual size)

EMBROIDERY POSITIONING DIAGRAM

INSTRUCTIONS

Read through all the instructions before you start to embroider.

If you wish to embroider the whole design, it's a good idea to start embroidering at the centre front first then work outwards to each side, beginning with the three large flowers.

If you're embroidering onto a garment, put it on then measure down from the neck edge. You need to leave a space of approx. 6cm / 2¼in above the embroidery, which is 12–14cm / 4¾–5½in deep. Place a stitch marker about 12cm / 4¾in below the neck opening at the centre-front of the garment. This marks the centre of the largest flower, where you will start the embroidery.

Remember to fasten off the threads as you go.

1. Flower no. 1: Use two strands of Lemon throughout. Start with the centre of the large flower in the middle of the embroidery. Embroider a circle outline of chain stitch about 2cm / ¾in in diameter. Fill the circle with chain stitch. Take care not to embroider too tightly. Keep an eye on this by checking that the stitches of the knitting don't twist or distort.

2. Around the chain-stitch centre, embroider the outlines of five petals also in chain stitch using two strands of Light Copper Brown. They don't all need to be the same size, but these stitches should lie firmly on the knitting. Note these outlines will be completely covered when the petals are filled in.

3. Now to fill the petals with colour, using vertical satin stitches. Every petal is divided into two horizontal sections, and one section is worked at a time. Start by embroidering the section closest to the centre of the flower with two strands of Light Copper Brown, which is roughly one-third of the length of the petal.

4. Fill in the second section of the petal with vertical satin stitches, again with two strands of Light Copper Brown. This section is roughly two-thirds of the length of the petal. Fill all the petals in the same way.

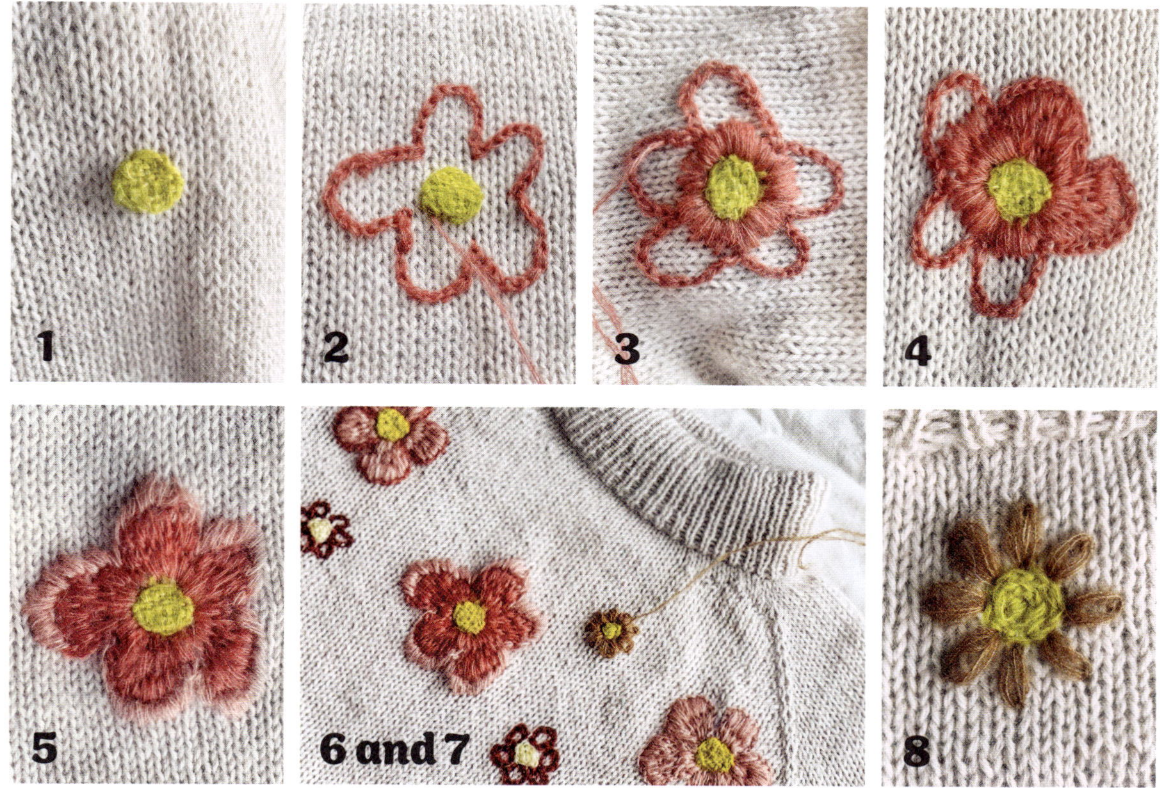

5. Using two strands of Powder Pink, embroider around the outer edge of the petal with vertical satin stitches. These stitches should cover the chain-stitch outline.

6. Now work two more flowers in the same way. Position these flowers either side of the central flower, a little higher so that the three flowers lie on a curve. (See the positioning diagram on page 23.) To vary the embroidery a little, work the last two flowers without the final area covering the chain stitches.

7. Flower no. 2 (the two dark flowers): Embroider the centre with two strands of Lime Punch in the same way described in step 1. Change to two strands of Deep Burgundy then work six circular outlines (the petals) in chain stitch around the Lime Punch centre, for the petals. The petals should be approx. the same size as the centre. As before, take care not to pull the thread too tight.

8. Flower no. 3: Start by embroidering a centre approx. 1–1.5cm / ½–⅝in in diameter with two strands of Lemon as described in step 1. Change to two strands of Light Acorn then embroider seven to eight petals around the Lemon centre using lazy daisy (detached chain) stitch. Each petal is made up of two lazy daisy (detached chain) stitches on top of another, and every stitch is approx. 2cm / ¾in long.

DO SHARE YOUR EMBROIDERY ON INSTAGRAM USING THE HASHTAG: #LOUGFEELSLIKESUMMER

9. Flower no. 4: This flower is a bit more demanding, as the centre is a French knot and the cast-on stitches are worked in curves around the centre. However, the effort is worth it as it'll produce an interesting 3D effect. Start by embroidering the centre in chain stitch with two strands of Lime Punch. Change to two strands of Tynn Silk Mohair in Powder Pink. Insert the needle into the work at the edge of the centre of the flower and bring it up again approx. 2cm / ¾in from the starting point, without pulling the needle through. Cast on eight to 12 loops around the needle. Hold onto the loops as you pull the needle and yarn through them. Tighten the yarn until the arc (petal) lies down nicely towards the centre. When you start on the next arc (petal), make sure it overlaps the first; to do this, you'll start by inserting the needle at around the middle of the first arc. Repeat as described above until you have four to five arcs of loops.

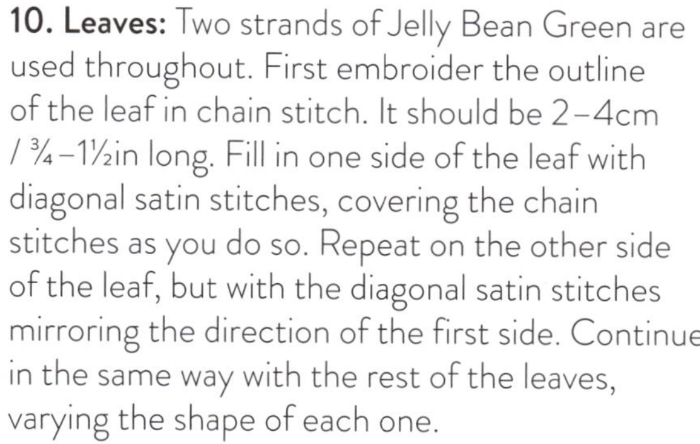

10. Leaves: Two strands of Jelly Bean Green are used throughout. First embroider the outline of the leaf in chain stitch. It should be 2–4cm / ¾–1½in long. Fill in one side of the leaf with diagonal satin stitches, covering the chain stitches as you do so. Repeat on the other side of the leaf, but with the diagonal satin stitches mirroring the direction of the first side. Continue in the same way with the rest of the leaves, varying the shape of each one.

Note: Flowers nos. 5 and 6 are used to fill the spaces between the flowers and leaves you have already embroidered, so they will vary in shape and size.

11. Flower no. 5: Start by working a centre approx. 1–1.5cm / ½–⅝in in diameter with chain stitch using two strands of Lime Punch. Change to two strands of Lemon then embroider simple straight stitches that radiate from the centre outwards.

12. Flower no. 6: Start by working a centre approx. 1–1.5cm / ½–⅝in in diameter with chain stitch using two strands of Lime Punch. For the petals, embroider lines of chain stitch using two strands of Plum Pink, radiating from the centre outwards and filling in the empty spaces between the other motifs.

9a 9b

10

11

12

They Say It's Spring

These pretty little flower buds are made in three colours, then embellished with a little gold thread. Although there is only one type of flower in this embroidery, you can rotate it in different directions to create variety. The flowers look wonderful worked all over the knitting, for a ditsy print effect.

Embroidery techniques

- Chain stitch
- Stem stitch
- Backstitch
- Straight stitch

Notions

- Long, thin, sharp yarn needle, with an eye large enough for thick yarn
- Scissors
- Embroidery frame (optional)
- Stitch markers
- A little gold thread, for embellishing

Yarn

Sandnes Garn: Kos
(62% alpaca, 29% nylon, 9% wool; chunky / bulky / weight 5; 50g / 150m / 164yd)

25g Light Sunny Lime 9512 (pale yellow-green)

25g Cognac 2745 (caramel)

25g Dusty Light Green 8521 (pale sage green)

INSTRUCTIONS

Read through all the instructions before you start to embroider.

Each flower has two leaves and a stem. Change the positioning of the stem and leaves to vary the angle of the flower. Start by inserting a stitch marker for each flower on the knitted piece. Spread them out and check if you are happy with the positioning. Take the markers out one by one as you embroider a flower.

1. Flower: Using one strand of Light Sunny Lime, work a single straight stitch approx. 1cm / ½in long (**1a**). Around this, embroider a circle of stem stitches, each stem stitch approx. 0.5–1cm / ¼–½in long (**1b**). Fasten off the threads on the wrong side of the work.

2. Stem: Starting from the flower and working outwards, embroider a stem in chain stitch using one strand of Cognac. The stem should be approx. 3cm / 1¼in long and will be made up of four to five slightly curving chain stitches. Vary the positioning slightly so that each flower faces a different way from the others close to it.

3. Leaves: On each side of the stem, embroider two straight stitches in Dusty Light Green. As for the stem, vary the direction and length of the leaves from flower to flower, so the flowers are not all the same.

4. To add a little pizzazz, finish by decorating a selection of flowers with a few stem stitches in gold thread. In the example on this page, I've embroidered along the base of the leaves, into one side of the flower bud and a part of the stem, but you can vary this.

Blessings

These dainty flowers, like dandelion clocks, are worked in three different stitches and colours. You don't need much of each shade, so you could embroider with left-over yarn in your favourite colours. They look very pretty when worked all over the knitting, as in the sample opposite.

Embroidery techniques

- French knot
- Backstitch
- Lazy daisy (detached chain) stitch

Notions

- Long, thin, sharp yarn needle
- Scissors
- Stitch markers
- Embroidery frame (optional)

Yarn

Sandnes Garn: Tynn Silk Mohair (57% mohair, 28% silk, 15% wool; 2-ply / lace / weight 0; 25g / 212m / 232yd)

25g Natural 1012 (off-white)

25g Light Copper Brown 3535 (rust)

25g Deep Blue 6081 (blueberry)

INSTRUCTIONS

Read through all the instructions before you start to embroider.

As the details on this flower are so small, they sit best on items worked with relatively small stitches and fine yarn, so the 'base' is as delicate as the flowers on it, and allows the flowers to shine.

Embroidering the flowers at slightly different angles adds variety. You can play with the leaf elements, too: add more or fewer leaves along the stem as desired.

You will need three colours, one for each part of the flower. Embroider with two strands of the same colour held together. Start by placing stitch markers on the knitting in the desired positions, to ensure a nicely balanced arrangement and spread of flowers. Always fasten off the loose ends each time you change thread. This will give the work a nice tidy back with no loops to catch accidentally.

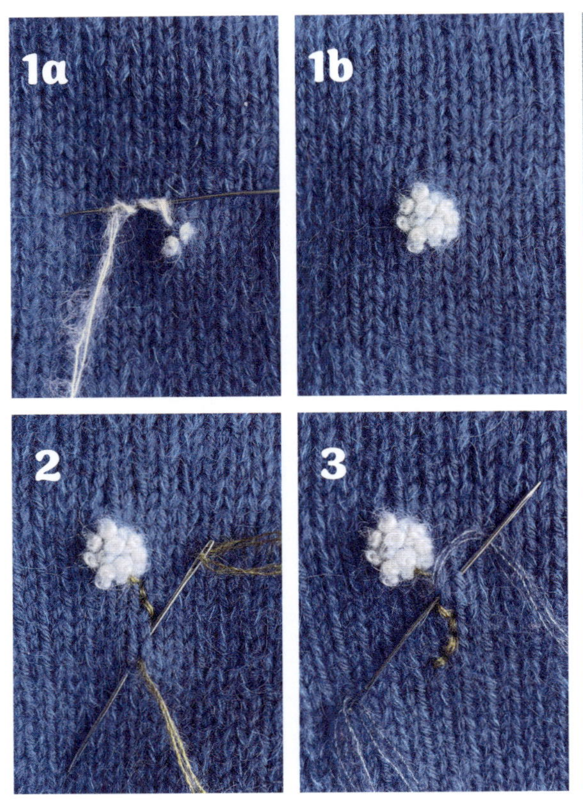

1. Flower: Using two strands of Natural, embroider a cluster of 15 to 16 French knots.

2. Stem: Using shade Light Copper Brown and working from the French-knot flower outwards, embroider a slightly curved line of backstitch approx. 3–4cm / 1¼–1½in long.

3. Leaves: Using Deep Blue, embroider a pair of lazy daisy (detached chain) stitches on each side of the stem. Leaving a little space between them, add two to three more pairs of leaves either side of the stem.

EMBROIDERY MOTIFS
(shown at actual size)

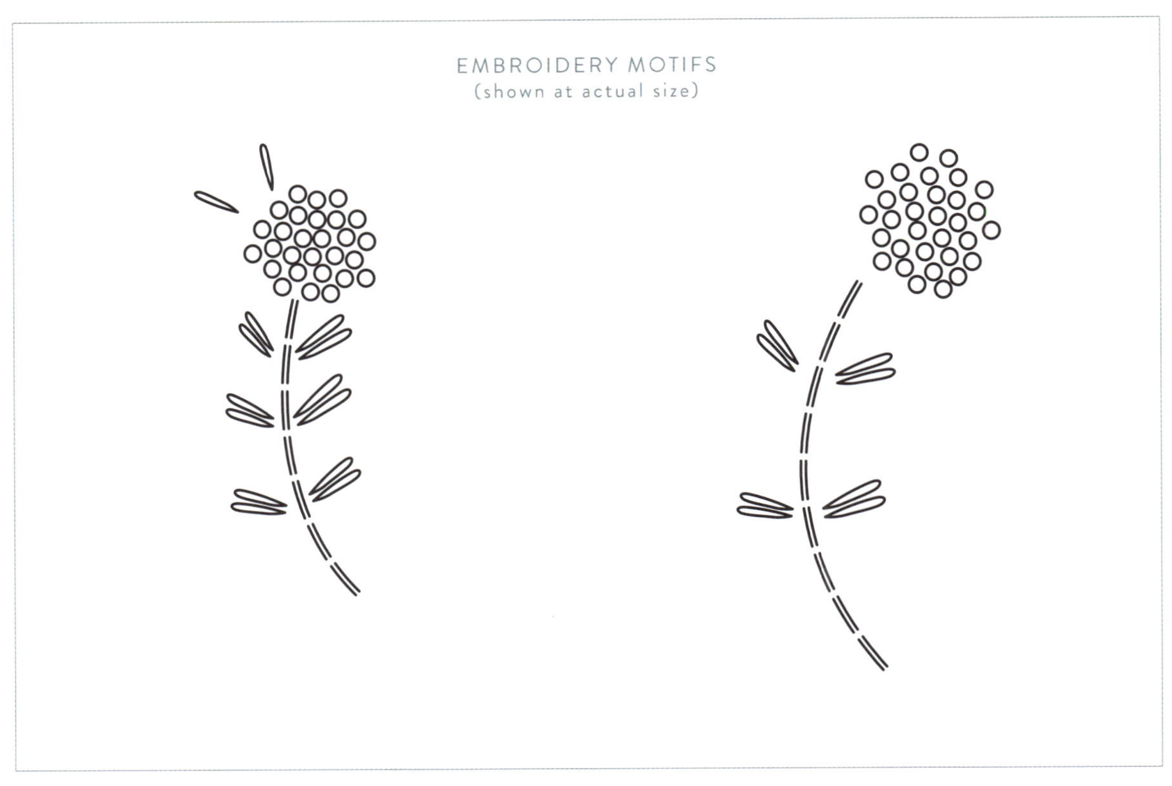

DO SHARE YOUR
EMBROIDERY ON
INSTAGRAM USING
THE HASHTAG:
#LOUGBLESSINGS

Colourful World

Here's a bright and bold statement embroidery! You can either stitch the whole design, or a few elements from it. The variety and size of the design will require some time and care. The embroidery is made with three kinds of yarn, in 14 colours overall.

Embroidery techniques

- Stem stitch
- Straight stitch
- Satin stitch
- Backstitch
- Chain stitch
- French knot

Yarn

Sandnes Garn: Ballerina Chunky Mohair (77% mohair, 18% wool, 5% nylon; chunky / bulky / weight 5; 50g / 135m / 148yd)

50g Coral Reef 3313 (pale bright orange)

Sandnes Garn: Kos (62% alpaca, 29% nylon, 9% wool; chunky / bulky / weight 5; 50g / 150m / 164yd)

50g Navy Blue 6079 (dark navy blue)

50g Dark Sky Blue 6042 (light steel blue)

50g Deep Burgundy 4372 (burgundy)

Sandnes Garn: Tynn Silk Mohair (57% mohair, 28% silk, 15% wool; 2-ply / lace / weight 0; 25g / 212m / 232yd)

25g Jelly Bean Green 8236 (bright green)

25g Powder Pink 3511 (blush pink)

25g Deep Red 4236 (crimson)

25g Deep Burgundy 4372 (burgundy)

25g Blossom 4213 (pink)

25g Almond 2511 (cream-brown)

25g Jolly Blue 6046 (bright blue)

25g Deep Blue 6081 (blueberry)

25g Dark Sky Blue 6042 (light steel blue)

25g Lemon 9004 (ice yellow)

Notions

- Two long, thin, sharp yarn needles – one for thin yarn and one for thick
- Scissors
- Stitch markers
- Embroidery frame

EMBROIDERY MOTIF
(shown at 30% actual size)

Numbers relate to steps on pages 43–45.

TSM = Tynn Silk Mohair
BCM = Ballerina Chunky Mohair

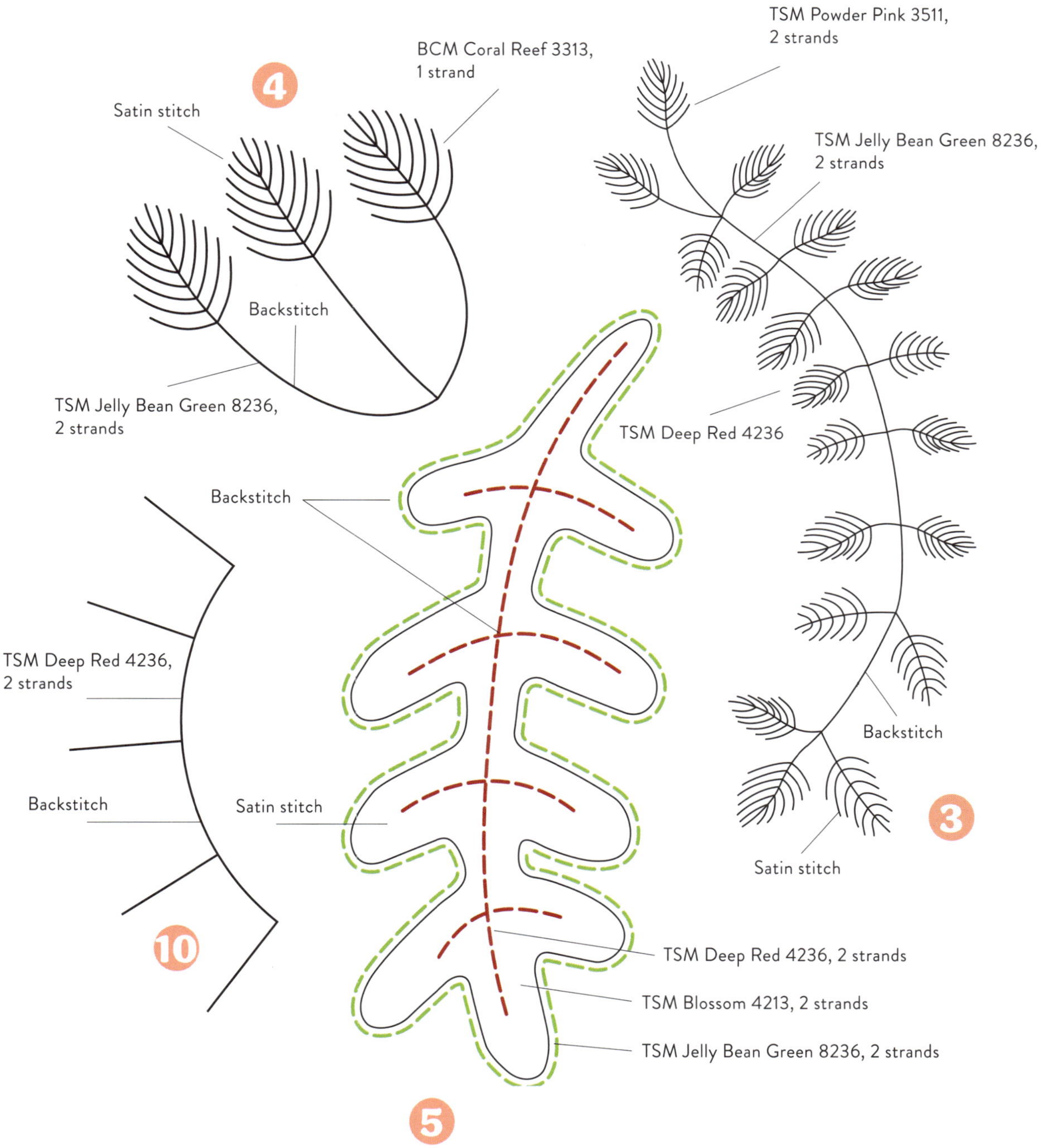

4

Satin stitch

BCM Coral Reef 3313, 1 strand

Backstitch

TSM Jelly Bean Green 8236, 2 strands

TSM Powder Pink 3511, 2 strands

TSM Jelly Bean Green 8236, 2 strands

TSM Deep Red 4236

Backstitch

3

Satin stitch

Backstitch

TSM Deep Red 4236, 2 strands

Backstitch

Satin stitch

10

TSM Deep Red 4236, 2 strands

TSM Blossom 4213, 2 strands

TSM Jelly Bean Green 8236, 2 strands

5

EMBROIDERY STITCHES AND COLOURS
(not actual size)

EMBROIDERY STITCHES AND COLOURS
(not actual size)

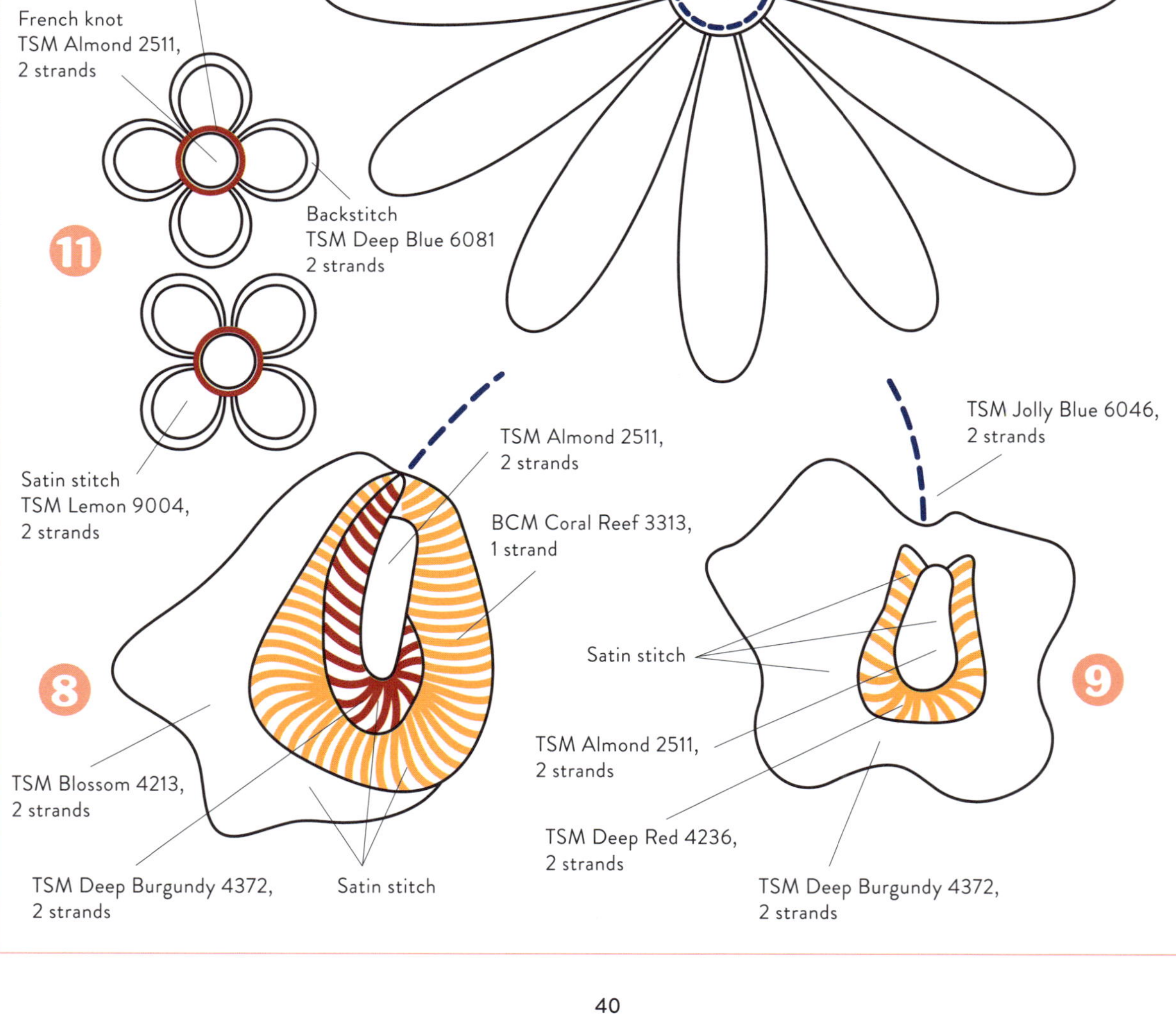

EMBROIDERY STITCHES AND COLOURS
(not actual size)

INSTRUCTIONS

Read through all the instructions before you start to embroider.

Embroidering over large areas is a little more demanding than working small motifs. It is very important that your stitches are not so tight that they pull the knitting together underneath – using an embroidery frame will help prevent this.

Start at the centre of the embroidery and work your way outwards. Similarly, always start at the centre of a flower and work outwards; this applies to all the flowers in the pattern. Place the flower in the middle of the embroidery (with the dark blue centre) at the centre front.

Remember to fasten off all the ends each time you change the thread.

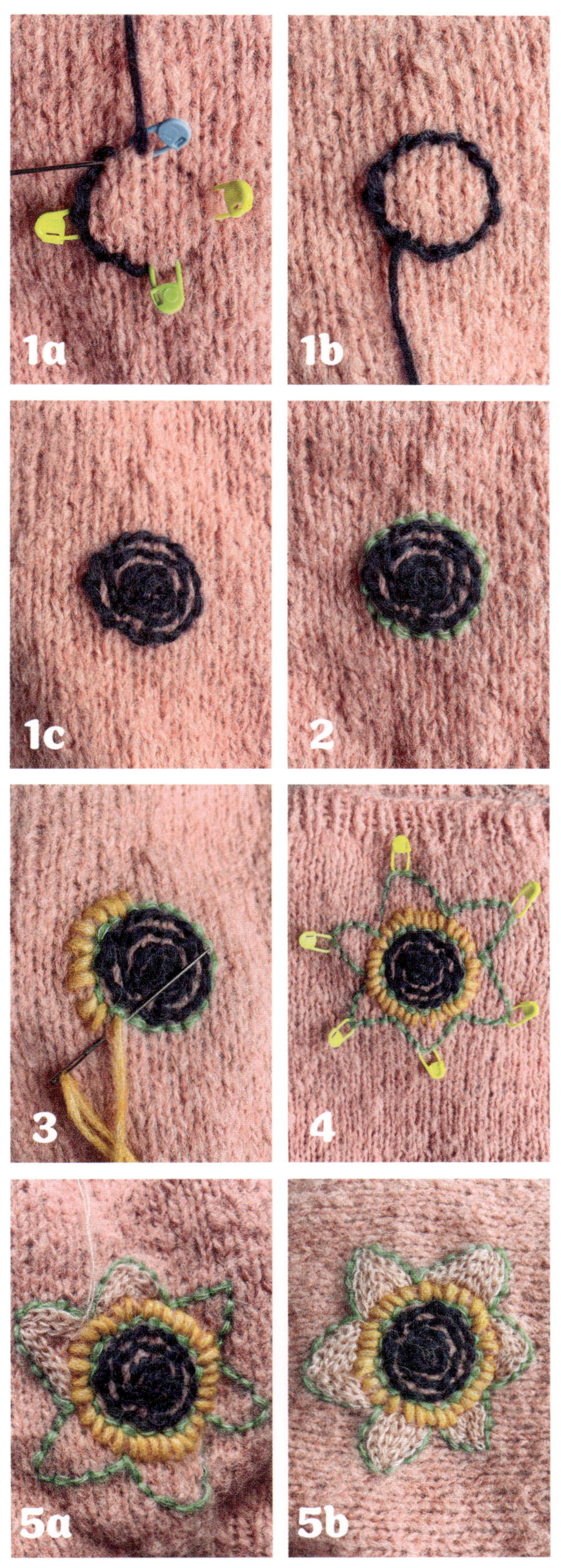

1. Central flower: Start with the dark blue centre of the dark blue flower in the middle of the knitting (numbered 1 in the diagrams on pages 38 and 41). Using one strand of Kos in Navy Blue, embroider an approx. 3.5–4cm / 1¼–1½in diameter circular outline in stem stitch. Then, working from the outside in, stitch more 'rings' of stem stitch to fill the centre. Take care to leave a very small distance between each ring; this is important as it ensures a nice, flat result. Fasten off the loose ends on the wrong side of the work.

2. Embroider a single ring of backstitch around the centre with two strands of Tynn Silk Mohair in Jelly Bean Green. Fasten off the ends.

3. Using one strand of Ballerina Chunky Mohair in Coral Reef, embroider vertical straight stitches around the green outline. Start each stitch approx. 1cm / ½in away from the green outline, and bring the needle out through the green outline. Turn the knitting as you go, so that the stitches radiate neatly from the centre – it is important to keep your eye on this, as they can easily curve to one side.

4. The petals for the flower are around 2cm / ¾in long at the highest point and 3cm / 1¼in wide. If you are embroidering freehand, you can place stitch markers in the knitted fabric to indicate the top of each petal, making sure they are evenly spaced – about 2cm / ¾in from the orange straight stitches. Embroider the outlines of the petals in backstitch with two strands of Tynn Silk Mohair in Jelly Bean Green.

5. Fill the petals with rounds of chain stitch using two strands of Tynn Silk Mohair in Powder Pink. Again, work from close to the centre outwards, and follow the shape of the petal for each 'round'.

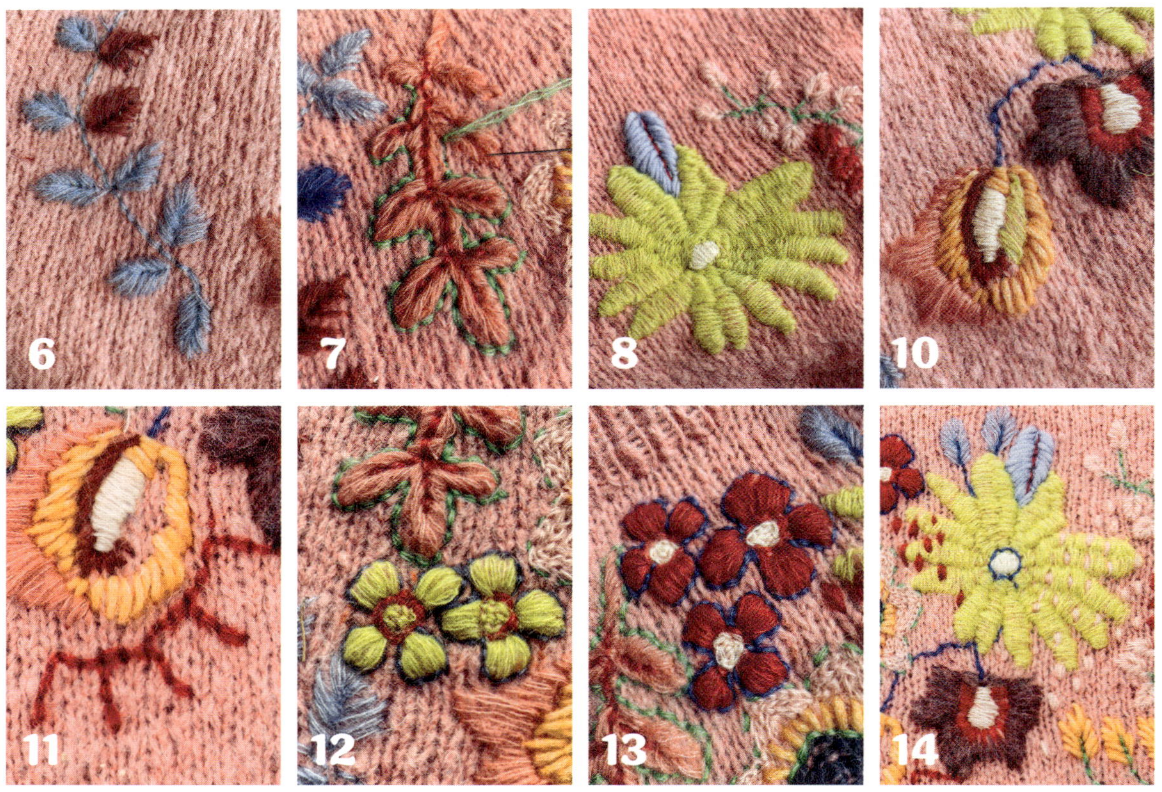

6. Simple leaves and leaf branches: Refer to the diagrams numbered 2, 3 and 4 on pages 38, 39 and 41 throughout for colours, stitches and positioning. Start with a stem embroidered in backstitch. The leaves are then stitched from the stem, with every leaf divided into two sections, with one half embroidered in diagonal satin stitches that 'point' in one direction, and the other half's diagonal satin stitches pointing in the other direction.

7. Large detailed leaf: Refer to the diagrams numbered 5 on pages 38 and 39 throughout. Embroider a stem with little branches in backstitch with two strands of Tynn Silk Mohair in Deep Red. Around the branches, but pointing away from them, embroider diagonal satin stitches with two strands of Tynn Silk Mohair in Blossom. Add diagonal satin stitches around the main stem too, again making sure they 'point' away from the stem. Finish the leaf by embroidering a backstitch outline all around the outer edges of the satin stitches with two strands of Tynn Silk Mohair in Jelly Bean Green.

DO SHARE YOUR EMBROIDERY ON INSTAGRAM USING THE HASHTAG: #LOUGCOLOURFULWORLD

8. Large yellow flower: Refer to the diagrams numbered 6 on pages 38 and 40 throughout. Embroider a circle approx. 2cm / ¾in in diameter with vertical satin stitches using two strands of Tynn Silk Mohair in Almond. From the centre, embroider approx. 12–15 petals with horizontal satin stitches using two strands of Tynn Silk Mohair in Lemon. For the wider petals, divide the petals into two tall sections, then embroider each half separately; this avoids too-long satin stitches. Finish the flower by embroidering backstitch around the centre with two strands of Tynn Silk Mohair in Jolly Blue.

9. Blue leaves above the large yellow flower: Refer to the diagrams numbered 7 on pages 38 and 40 throughout. Stitch one leaf at a time. Above the top petals of the large yellow flower, embroider diagonal satin stitches that radiate out from invisible stems – for the left-hand and middle stems use two strands of Tynn Silk Mohair in Dark Sky Blue, and for the right-hand stem use one strand of Kos in Dark Sky Blue. To finish each leaf, backstitch a line between the radiating diagonal stitches of each leaf, using two strands of Tynn Silk Mohair – the left-hand and middle stems with Jolly Blue, and the right-hand stem in Deep Red. This makes the stem more prominent and helps to secure the satin stitches to your knitted base too.

10. Centre-bottom flowers: Refer to the diagrams numbered 8 and 9 on pages 38 and 40 throughout. Stitch one flower at a time. Embroider a 2–3cm / ¾–1¼in ovular-shaped centre in satin stitch with two strands of Tynn Silk Mohair in Almond. Then, embroider the rest of the flowerheads in satin stitch, referring to the diagrams for colours and placement. Complete the flowers by backstitching stems that join and 'disappear' behind the large yellow flower using two strands of Tynn Silk Mohair in Jolly Blue.

11. Eyelash motif: Refer to the diagrams numbered 10 on pages 38 and 39 throughout. Simply embroider the whole motif with only backstitch using two strands of Tynn Silk Mohair in Deep Red.

12. Small bottom-left yellow flowers: Refer to the diagrams numbered 11 on pages 38 and 40 throughout. Stitch one flower at a time. Start by stitching a cluster of four-wrap French knots for the centre of each flower using two strands of Tynn Silk Mohair in Lemon, creating a centre that is approx. 1cm / ½in in diameter. With the same number of strands and colour, from the centre of each flower embroider four petals using vertical satin stitches. The petals should be approx. 1cm / ½in tall. All around the French-knot centre, backstitch an outline using two strands of Tynn Silk Mohair in Deep Red. To finish, embroider an outline around the petals of each flower in backstitch using two strands of Tynn Silk Mohair in Deep Blue.

13. Small centre-top red flowers: Referring to the diagrams numbered 12 on pages 38 and 41 throughout, follow the same process described in step 12 to stitch the flowers. Note that the backstitch outline around the French-knot centre uses the same colour as the satin-stitched petals.

14. Accents: To finish, 'scatter' vertical straight stitches over the left and bottom-right areas of the large yellow flower. Each straight stitch is made up of two layers of two strands of Tynn Silk Mohair (the left area uses Deep Red, the bottom-right area uses Powder Pink), and the overall shape of each area's straight stitches resembles raindrops.

The Rose

This rose is a tribute to the classic flower, with a modern twist. In the sample opposite, the roses are worked in one yarn – Tynn Silk Mohair – using chain stitch and satin stitch, and tone with the colour of the sweater.

Embroidery stitches

- Chain stitch
- Satin stitch

Notions

- Long, thin, sharp yarn needle
- Scissors
- Stitch markers
- Embroidery frame (optional)

Yarn

Sandnes Garn: Tynn Silk Mohair (57% mohair, 28% silk, 15% wool; lace /weight 0; 25g / 212m / 232yd)

25g Blossom 4213 (pink)

INSTRUCTIONS

Read through all the instructions before you start to embroider.

The whole design is worked using two strands of the same yarn, and in the same colour.

Since the initial outline is relatively detailed, I recommend using the water-soluble paper method for transferring the outlines to your knitting, before stitching – see page 10 for more information.

Embroider each rose in turn. Fasten off all the ends as you go for a nice, tidy wrong side, and to prevent you snagging previously worked stitches.

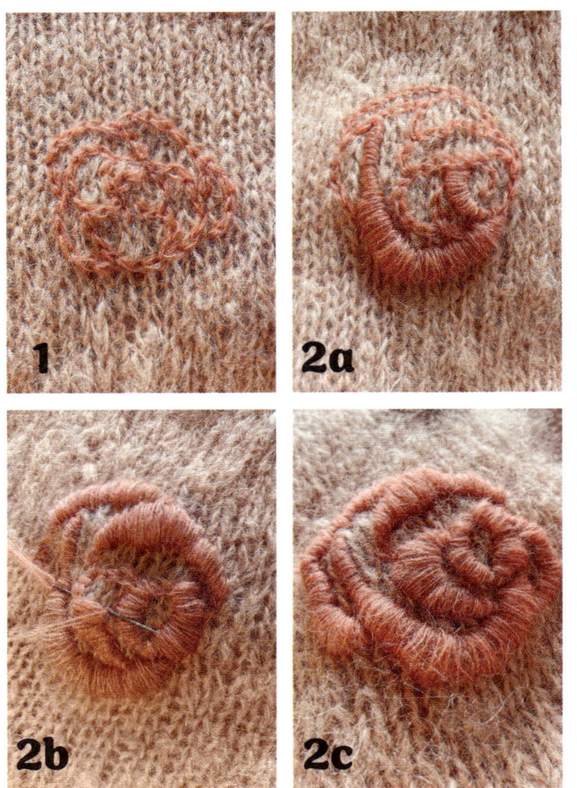

1. Embroider the outline of the rose in chain stitch (see the diagram below). Start at the centre with the 2cm / ¾in curve then work outwards until the flower measures approx. 10cm / 4in. The chain stitches help to stabilize the embroidery.

2. Referring to the diagram below again, fill in the areas between the curves with satin stitch, sewing over the chain stitches to hide them (**2a** and **2b**). Take care not to pull the thread too tight or make the embroidery too dense – an embroidery hoop will help with this. Your stitches should follow the curve. This helps to make the rose more lifelike (**2c**).

EMBROIDERY MOTIF
(shown at actual size)

DO SHARE YOUR EMBROIDERY ON INSTAGRAM USING THE HASHTAG: #LOUGTHEROSE

I Got Stripes

Sometimes, a simple design is all you need. These stripes are created with duplicate stitch, and look effective when embroidered partway down the centre of the sweater sleeves, as seen in the sample opposite.

Embroidery techniques

- Duplicate stitch

Notions

- Long, thin, blunt yarn needle, with an eye large enough for thick yarn
- Scissors

Yarn

Sandnes Garn: Kos
(62% alpaca, 29% nylon, 9% wool;
chunky / bulky / weight 5;
50g / 150m / 164yd)

50g Beige 3532 (cream-brown)

50g Navy Blue 6079 (dark navy blue) – this is for the variation shown on page 53.

INSTRUCTIONS

Read through all the instructions before you start to embroider.

The design consists of simple stripes stacked on top of each other, embroidered with duplicate stitch. I recommend starting with the top-most stripe first, then use this as a guide to work the rest below it.

Fasten off ends after working each stripe, to keep the wrong side neat.

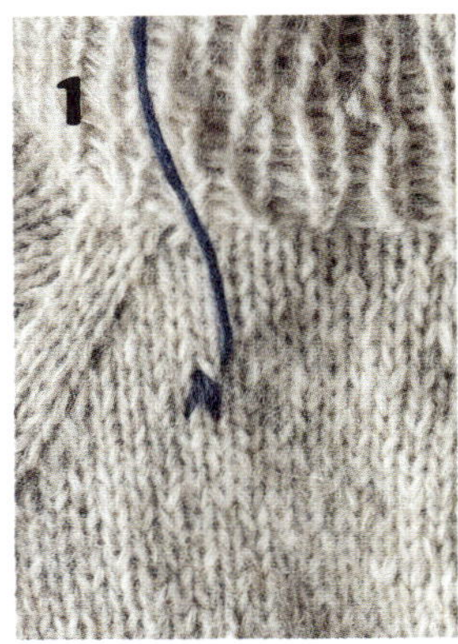

1. First stripe: Find the centre-top of the area to be embroidered – this gives you the centre line to work out from. Count four knit stitches out from this centre line, on each side, then embroider all eight stitches in the row with duplicate stitch (so eight duplicate stitches in total). Note that the number of stitches here is based on a knitted piece made with chunky (bulky / weight 5) yarn; you may need to add or reduce the number of stitches if your yarn weight is different.

2. Embroider another row of duplicate stitches below the first row. You now have two rows of duplicate stitches, one above the other. This constitutes one stripe.

3. Other stripes: count four rounds down from the bottom of the first stripe. Start the next stripe at the outer edge and embroider another stripe in the same way.

4. Repeat until you have embroidered 10 stripes in total.

5. If stitching onto a garment's sleeves, as seen in the samples left and opposite, embroider the second sleeve in the same way.

6. Fasten off the loose ends on the wrong side of the knitting.

DO SHARE YOUR EMBROIDERY ON INSTAGRAM USING THE HASHTAG: #LOUGIGOTSTRIPES

The embroidery on the beige sweater is worked in Sandnes Garn Kos: Navy Blue 6079.

Better With You

This is a large, detailed embroidery with stunning colourful flowers made in two different yarns. The small beads at the centres of the smaller flowers are subtle, pretty details that give the design that little bit extra.

Embroidery techniques

- Chain stitch
- Backstitch
- Satin stitch
- Straight stitch

Notions

- Two long, thin, sharp yarn needles – one for thin yarn and one for thick
- Scissors
- Embroidery frame (optional, but it can be a great help to give you a taut and stable surface to embroider on, and stops you pulling the embroidery thread too tight)
- Stitch markers (optional)
- Small beads to fill the centres of the smaller flowers

Yarn

Sandnes Garn: Kos
(62% alpaca, 29% nylon, 9% wool; chunky / bulky / weight 5; 50g / 150m / 164yd)

50g Dark Sky Blue 6042 (pale steel blue)

50g Beige 3532 (cream-brown)

Sandnes Garn: Tynn Silk Mohair
(57% mohair, 28% silk, 15% wool; 2-ply / lace / weight 0; 25g / 212m / 232yd)

10–15g Jelly Bean Green 8236 (bright green)

25g Powder Pink 3511 (blush pink)

10–15g Deep Red 4236 (crimson)

10–15g Jolly Blue 6046 (bright blue)

10g Natural 1012 (off-white)

FLOWER NO. 1
(shown at actual size)

TSM = Tynn Silk Mohair

Backstitch,
TSM Deep Red 4236,
2 strands

Satin stitch
TSM Jelly Bean Green 8236,
2 strands

Satin stitch
Kos Beige 3532, 1 strand

Backstitch
TSM Jolly Blue 6046,
2 strands

Satin stitch
Kos Beige 3532,
1 strand

Satin stitch
TSM Powder Pink 3511,
2 strands

Satin stitch
Kos Dark Sky Blue 6042,
1 strand

Backstitch,
TSM Deep Red 4236,
2 strands

FLOWER NO. 2
(shown at actual size)

FLOWER NO. 3
(shown at actual size)
Satin stitch
TSM Natural 1012,
2 strands
Satin stitch
TSM Jelly Bean Green 8236,
2 strands
Satin stitch
Kos Beige 3532, 1 strand
Backstitch
TSM Deep Red 4236, 2 strands
No stitching
(knitting showing through)
Satin stitch
TSM Powder Pink 3511, 2 strands
Satin stitch
Kos Beige 3532, 1 strand
OTHER FLORAL DETAILS
(shown at actual size)
Straight stitch
Kos Dark Sky Blue 6042, 1 strand
Backstitch
Kos Dark Sky Blue 6042, 1 strand
Satin stitch
TSM Powder Pink 3511, 2 strands
Chain stitch
TSM Powder Pink 3511, 2 strands
Straight stitch
TSM Deep Red 4236, 2 strands

INSTRUCTIONS

Read through all the instructions before you start to embroider.

This may not be the simplest embroidery, but with a little patience – and perhaps some practise on a swatch to start with – you'll be able to manage it. The most important and perhaps the most difficult thing about embroidering across a large area is to avoid pulling the stitches so tight that the knitting puckers. You can use an embroidery frame to help prevent this.

The design consists of three main flowers: one central flower with two more flowers either side of it, both a little lower down so they are not all in a straight line. Between the flowers are leaves in the same colour as the centre of the larger flower, plus a few small flowers that complement the pinks in the left- and right-hand flowers.

1. Outlines: I recommend using the water-soluble paper method to transfer the outlines on pages 56–58 onto the knitting; this will give you a good starting point for the positioning and size of the flowers, and make it easier when placing the stitches too. If you prefer to embroider freehand, place stitch markers in the knitting to mark the centres of the flowers; these will serve as points of reference when embroidering.

2. Embroider the outlines in chain stitch with a thin waste yarn or thread. The chain stitches will stabilize the embroidery and be completely hidden in the end, so don't worry about what the stitches look like. Choose a colour that is a little like the colour you will be using to fill the petals of the flower. Use quite long stitches, approx. 1cm / ½in long, so they don't disappear into the spaces between the stitches of the knitting. After the outlines are established, wash away the water-soluble paper.

3. Flower no. 1: Start at the innermost part of the central flower and work your way outwards, filling each area, one by one, with satin stitch. Refer to the diagram on page 56 for information on stitches and colours to use. It's very important that the stitches are not worked too closely together, or pulled too tight, to prevent the knitting getting pulled out of shape. The stitches should cover the chain stitches, so always take the needle down over the chain-stitch outlines.

4. Flower nos. 2 and 3: Embroider these in the same way, referring to the diagrams on pages 57 and 58 for information on stitches and colours to use.

5. Green leaves around Flower nos. 1–3: Refer to the diagrams on pages 56–58 if needed, and use two strands of Tynn Silk Mohair throughout. With shade Deep Red, embroider the veins in backstitch. Around the veins, and with the stitches running perpendicular to them, embroider satin stitch in shade Jelly Bean Green.

6. Small flowers: Place a few small flowers in between the large main flowers – use stitch markers to start with, to help decide placement. Using two strands of Tynn Silk Mohair in Powder Pink, embroider a ring with chain stitch. The ring should be about 0.5cm / ¼in in diameter; this is the centre of the flower.

7. Working outwards from the chain-stitch ring, and with the same yarn and colour, embroider five petals for each flower with five to six satin stitches. For each petal, the central stitch needs to be taller than the outer stitches, and measure approx. 2cm / ¾in long. Lastly, embroider a single straight stitch from the centre and out over the middle of each of the petal with two strands of Tynn Silk Mohair in Deep Red.

8. Small blue leaves between large flowers: These fill the gaps between the small and large flowers, and can be in small clusters or on their own. Refer to the diagrams on page 58 if needed, and use one strand of Kos in Dark Sky Blue throughout. Start by stitching the central vein in backstitch, its length measuring approx. 3–4cm / 1¼–1½in long. Then, embroider diagonal straight stitches on each side of the vein. Work each side in turn, and take care to leave a small distance between the stitches.

DO SHARE YOUR EMBROIDERY ON INSTAGRAM USING THE HASHTAG: #LOUGBETTERWITHYOU

Flower Power 1

These large, retro flowers add a subtle pop of fun to bags, sofa pillow covers, sweaters and more. The flowers are worked in three colours and two weights of yarn. The design is a slightly more subdued version of the Flower Power 2 embroidery, on page 90.

Embroidery techniques

- Satin stitch
- Chain stitch
- Backstitch

Yarn

Sandnes Garn: Alpakka Ull (65% alpaca, 35% wool; aran / worsted / weight 4; 50g / 100m / 109yd)

50g Cognac 2745 (caramel brown)

Sandnes Garn: Tynn Silk Mohair (57% mohair, 28% silk, 15% wool; 2-ply / lace / weight 0; 25g / 212m / 232yd)

25g Natural 1012 (off-white)

25g Jelly Bean Green 8236 (bright green)

Notions

- Two long, thin, sharp yarn needles – one for thin yarn and one for thick
- Scissors
- Stitch markers

INSTRUCTIONS

Read through all the instructions before you start to embroider.

The flowers are about 9–10cm / 3½–4in in diameter, with a centre of approx. 3cm / 1¼in. Use the same embroidery pattern as a reference throughout. Place a stitch marker for every flower on the knitting before you start, to ensure you end up with a nice spread. Fasten off all the ends as you go; this will help you to keep the back nice and tidy.

1. Centre: Using two strands of Tynn Silk Mohair in Jelly Bean Green, embroider an approx. 3cm / 1¼in diameter ring with chain stitch. (See page 92 for step-by-step photographs illustrating how to embroider a flower like this.)

2. Working inside the chain-stitched outline, fill the inside of the ring with satin stitches using two strands of Tynn Silk Mohair in Natural.

3. Petals: Tack / baste the outlines of the petals around the chain-stitch centre with one strand of Tynn Silk Mohair in Natural, to use as your guide lines.

4. Using two strands of Tynn Silk Mohair in Natural throughout, and working each petal in turn, fill the tacked / basted petal outlines with satin stitch. To fill the petals, first divide each petal into two equal horizontal sections. Then, embroider the first section – the area close to the centre – with a row of satin stitches, followed by the second section close to the outer edge of the petal. Working this way ensures the stitches won't being too long. Embroider the satin stitches for the second section over the tacked / basted outline. Take care not to embroider too tightly; the stitches should lie flat beside each other.

5. Outlines: Embroider around the edges of the petals in chain stitch using two strands of Tynn Silk Mohair in Jelly Bean Green. It is important not to pull the stitches too tight. Pull the end of the thread through gently until the loops lie close to the knitting.

6. Last of all, embroider a second ring around and outside the centre of the flower, this time in backstitch using one strand of Alpakka Ull in Cognac.

EMBROIDERY MOTIF
(shown at actual size)

Adore You

The flowery design, made with just two techniques and in one yarn and one colour, involves stitching a stunning cluster of flowers around the desired area of your knitting – in the sweater opposite, the embroidery motif wraps around the upper yoke and bottom of the sleeves. There's a lovely feminine feel to this design, and it would beautifully patch up a worn part of a beloved knitted garment.

Embroidery techniques

- Lazy daisy (detached chain) stitch
- French knot

Notions

- Long, thin, sharp yarn needle, with an eye large enough for thick yarn
- Scissors
- Embroidery frame (optional)

Yarn

Sandnes Garn: Kos
(62% alpaca, 29% nylon, 9% wool; chunky / bulky / weight 5; 50g / 150m / 164yd)

50g Natural 1012 (off-white)

INSTRUCTIONS

Read through all the instructions before you start to embroider.

I've created this design so it can 'cluster' around the edge (or edges) of an item, then follow the shape of whatever it is stitched on. For a more organic appearance, allow a few of the flowers to extend beyond the denser cluster.

I recommend marking out and stitching the large flowers first, to give you the key shapes to work from and ensure an even design; you can then fill the spaces between the larger flowers with smaller ones.

Always embroider one flower at a time, and fasten off when you've finished working each type of stitch. The flowers are embroidered with a single strand of yarn throughout.

1. Large flowers: Each flower is approx. 7cm / 2¾in in diameter. Start with a large flower in the middle of the area you wish to add the design to. Begin with the centre of the flower: make a cluster of eight or so three-wrap French knots, embroidering them as close together as you can. The diameter of the centre should be 1.5–2cm / ½–¾in.

2. Each petal is embroidered with two lazy daisy (detached chain) stitches, one on top of the other and measuring approx. 2–2.5cm / ¾–1in long. There are eight petals in total, and they sit in a 'ring' around the French knots. Start with the top petal which points straight up, then stitch the bottom petal which points straight down. Add a petal to the left- and right-hand edges, then finally add petals in the gaps between all these petals. (Refer to the A–H order in the diagram opposite.)

3. Repeat to add the remaining desired number of large flowers.

4. Small flowers: Now fill in the spaces between the large flowers with smaller flowers. The size and shape of these flowers, and the number of petals they have, will depend on the space they sit in; but, otherwise, they are made in a similar way to the large flowers. Start with the centre, embroidering a group of three or four three-wrap French knots to form a circle. Then embroider the petals with a double layer of lazy daisy (detached chain) stitches around the cluster of French knots. Note that you may only have room to add only five or six petals. Extend the petals as far as you can, towards the neighbouring large flowers but without overlapping them.

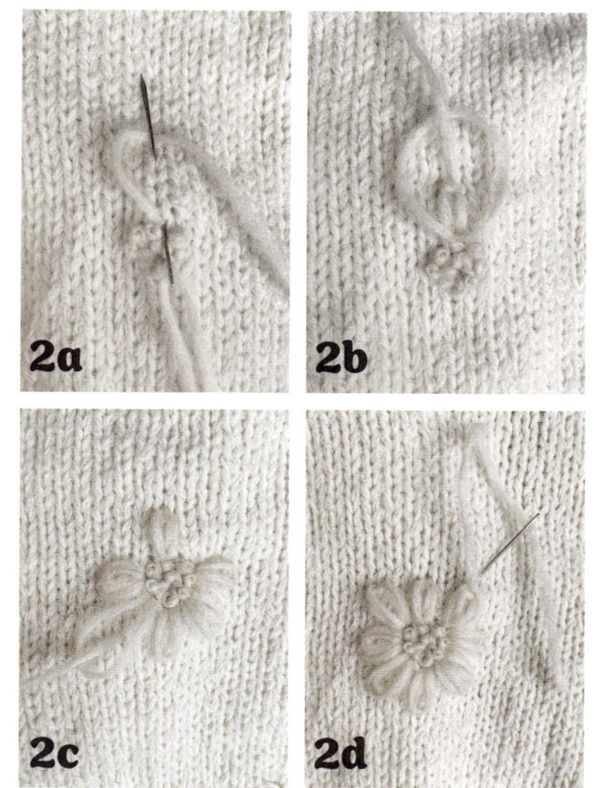

DO SHARE YOUR EMBROIDERY ON INSTAGRAM USING THE HASHTAG: #LOUGADOREYOU

Are You Ready

A row of flowers looks fabulous along the edge of a shawl, or across the chest of a sweater, as seen in the sample opposite. These are simple yet bold stalked flowers, made in two colours.

Embroidery techniques

- Lazy daisy (detached chain) stitch
- Chain stitch
- French knot (optional)

Notions

- Long, thin, sharp yarn needle, with an eye large enough for thick yarn
- Scissors
- Stitch markers

Yarn

HipKnitShop: Fluff
(80% kid mohair, 11% merino wool, 9% polyamide; chunky / bulky / weight 5; 50g / 100m / 109¼yd)

50g Berrylicious (cherry red)

50g Champagne (ochre)

INSTRUCTIONS

Read through all the instructions before you start to embroider.

To embroider your flowers in a neat row, it's important to measure and mark to start with.

There should be approximately 10–11cm / 4–4¼in between each flower, measured from centre to centre. Start the design by placing a stitch marker for the first flower at the centre of the area to be embroidered; you'll then work from this central flower.

Fasten off ends as you work, to keep the back neat and to avoid snagging previously worked embroidery stitches.

1. Stalk: Working vertically, and from the bottom upwards, embroider a stalk in chain stitch using two strands of Fluff in Champagne. You should have six chain stitches in total.

2. Leaves: Start in the second chain stitch down from the top. Bring the needle up from the wrong side of the knitting in the middle of the chain stitch then embroider a sideways lazy daisy (detached chain) stitch out to the side (**2a**). The stitch should be approx. 1.5cm / ⅝in long. Work another stitch on top (**2b**), so there is a double layer of lazy daisy (detached chain) stitches. One leaf made. Embroider a second leaf in the same way on the opposite side, creating a pair of leaves. Repeat to embroider a second pair of leaves two chain stitches below (**2c**).

3. Centre (optional): If desired, work a two-wrap French knot with Fluff in Champagne, above the top chain stitch.

4. Flower: Refer to the embroidery diagrams opposite for guidance if necessary. Use two strands of Fluff in Berrylicious throughout. Every petal should be worked from the centre outwards, and each petal is made with a double layer of lazy daisy (detached chain) stitches. Start with the two horizontal petals, then embroider the two diagonal petals that point downwards. Finish by stitching two diagonal petals that point upwards. Fasten off the loose ends. You have now finished the petals for the first flower.

5. Repeat until you have a ring of flowers all the way round the yoke.

DO SHARE YOUR EMBROIDERY ON INSTAGRAM USING THE HASHTAG: #LOUGAREYOUREADY

EMBROIDERY MOTIF
(shown at actual size)

EMBROIDERY WORKING DIAGRAM FOR FLOWER
(not actual size)

Flowers with French-knot centre

Counting Stars

Cover the whole of your knitting in a grid of stars! The stars are easy to embroider and are finished with a little French knot in the middle in a contrasting colour, for extra texture and interest.

Embroidery techniques

- Straight stitch
- French knot

Notions

- Long, thin, sharp yarn needle, with an eye large enough for thick yarn
- Scissors
- Stitch markers

Yarn

Sandnes Garn: Kos
(62% alpaca, 29% nylon, 9% wool; chunky / bulky / weight 5; 50g / 150m / 164yd)

50g Navy Blue 6079 (dark navy blue)

50g Cognac 2745 (caramel)

INSTRUCTIONS

Read through all the instructions before you start to embroider.

The stars are easy to embroider; it's just a matter of ensuring the distance between them is consistent throughout. There should be approximately 10–11cm / 4–4¼in between each star.

To mark star placements, begin with a star in the centre of your knit, then working outwards to the left and to the right to complete the row. Then, use this row as a guide for distance and placement for the remaining stars.

Fasten off all the loose ends as you go along; this will give the knitting a nice tidy back with no loops that your embroidery needle could catch by accident.

1. Start by embroidering the main star shape with one strand of Kos in Navy Blue. Bring the needle and thread up from the wrong side in the middle of the knit stitch. Leave a tail of approx. 10cm / 4in on the wrong side to fasten off with after you have embroidered the star.

2. Take the needle down through the knitting to the right, approx. 1cm / ⅜in away, then bring the needle up again at the starting point.

3. Sew another horizontal straight stitch of the same length to the left, and again bring the needle up at the starting point.

4. Sew a vertical straight stitch above the centre point, taking the needle down through the knitting approx. 1cm / ⅜in away, and bringing it back up again at the starting point. Try to 'lock' the stitch in place by bringing the needle up though the fibres of the horizontal stitches.

5. Sew a vertical stitch below the centre point in the same way and at the same length. You should now have a cross shape.

6. Sew a diagonal stitch between each 'spoke' of the cross shape, again approx. 1cm / ⅜in long – it doesn't matter which one you do first. As you pull the needle through, support the embroidery with your fingers on both sides of the knitting, so you don't pull on the stitches too much and distort the star or fabric. The centre of the star will be 'locked' in place when you sew through the fibres from an earlier stitch. Finish by fastening off both ends of the thread at the back of the star. Sew a couple of stitches on the back and cut the thread.

7. Change to Kos in Cognac. Embroider a small, three-wrap French knot in the centre of the star. Fasten off both ends.

8. Continue embroidering stars in the same way, leaving a gap of approx. 10–11cm / 4–4¼in between each star.

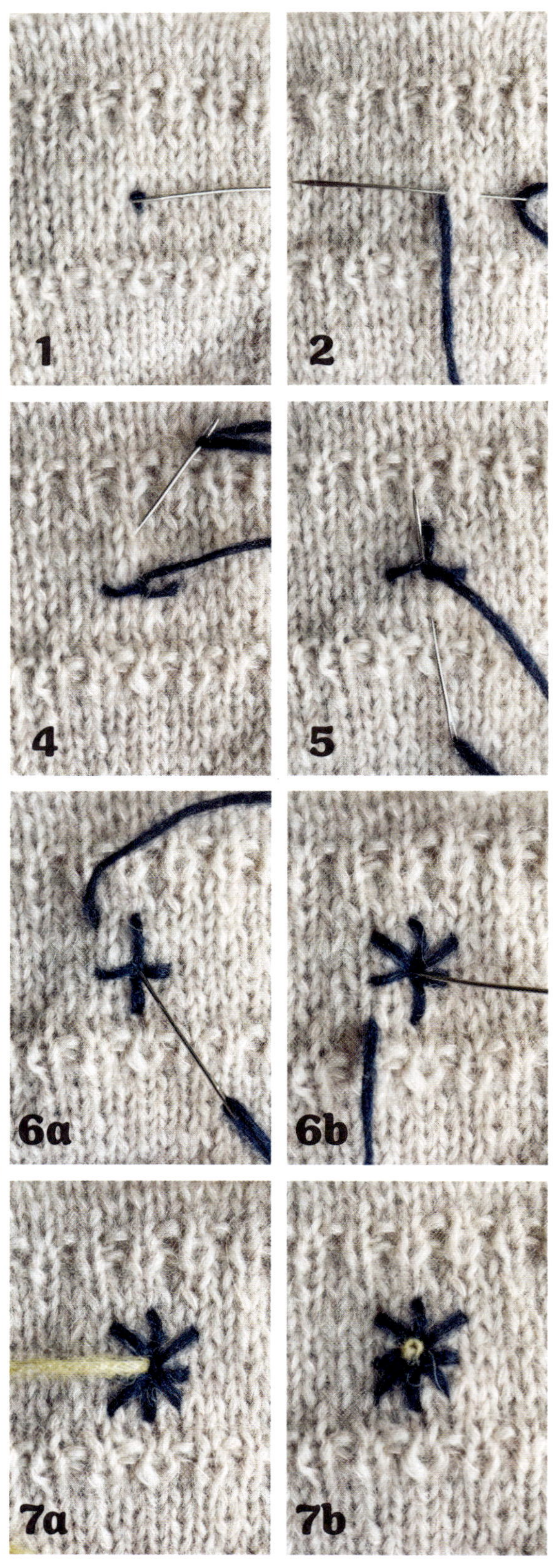

EMBROIDERY MOTIF AND WORKING DIAGRAMS
(shown at actual size)
DO SHARE YOUR EMBROIDERY ON INSTAGRAM USING THE HASHTAG: #LOUGCOUNTINGSTARS

Heart To Heart

These fun satin-stitched hearts can be playfully embroidered over a blanket or sweater in a random fashion. In my opinion, the more colours the better! But, equally, a single colour does look stunning. This is a perfect design for using up a collection of leftovers from your stash.

Embroidery stitches

- Backstitch
- Satin stitch

Yarn

HipKnitShop: Hip Wool (100% Peruvian Highland Wool; Aran / worsted / weight 4; 50g / 80m / 87½yd)

50g Dancing Snowflake White (off-white)

50g Dusty Candyfloss Pink (pale pink)

50g I'm Blushing (warm rose pink)

50g Yummy Honey Yellow (pale yellow)

50g Falling For You Blue (bright blue)

HipKnitShop: Hip Mohair (80% mohair, 20% polyamide; lace / 2-ply / weight 0; 25g / 210m / 229½yd)

25g Cotton Ball White (white)

25g Candyfloss (pale pink)

25g Raspberry Pink (raspberry pink)

25g Here Comes The Sun (bright yellow)

25g Bubbly Blue (bright blue)

Notions

- Two long, thin, sharp yarn needles – one for thin yarn and one for thick
- Scissors
- Embroidery frame (optional)

INSTRUCTIONS

Read through all the instructions before you start to embroider.

The cute little hearts, about 3.5–4cm / 1⅜–1½in in height, are embroidered in two yarns of different thicknesses. The hearts are embroidered in two steps: work the outline first, then 'fill' it with stripes of colour.

Mark where you want to place the hearts on your knit with stitch markers. I like a random approach, but do ensure they're still somewhat evenly spread throughout the knit. Remember, you will start the heart outline from the bottom point, so consider this when thinking about where to place your stitch markers.

Fasten off all the ends as you go; this will prevent stitches snagging on the back.

1. Outline: With two strands of your chosen-colour of Hip Mohair yarn, bring the needle up from the wrong side of the work where you have placed the marker. Embroider the outline of the heart in backstitch, working from the bottom tip, around the two curves then back to the tip.

2. Filling: Use one strand of coordinating Hip Wool throughout, and referring to the embroidery pattern diagrams opposite, work three or four stitches in satin stitch on one half of the heart. They should be close to each other, and slope diagonally from the left-hand curved top towards the pointed bottom tip.

3. Repeat step 2 on the other side of the heart, with the satin stitches sloping in the opposite direction and overlapping the previous stitches at the bottom of the heart. One completed heart.

4. Continue as above for the rest of the hearts.

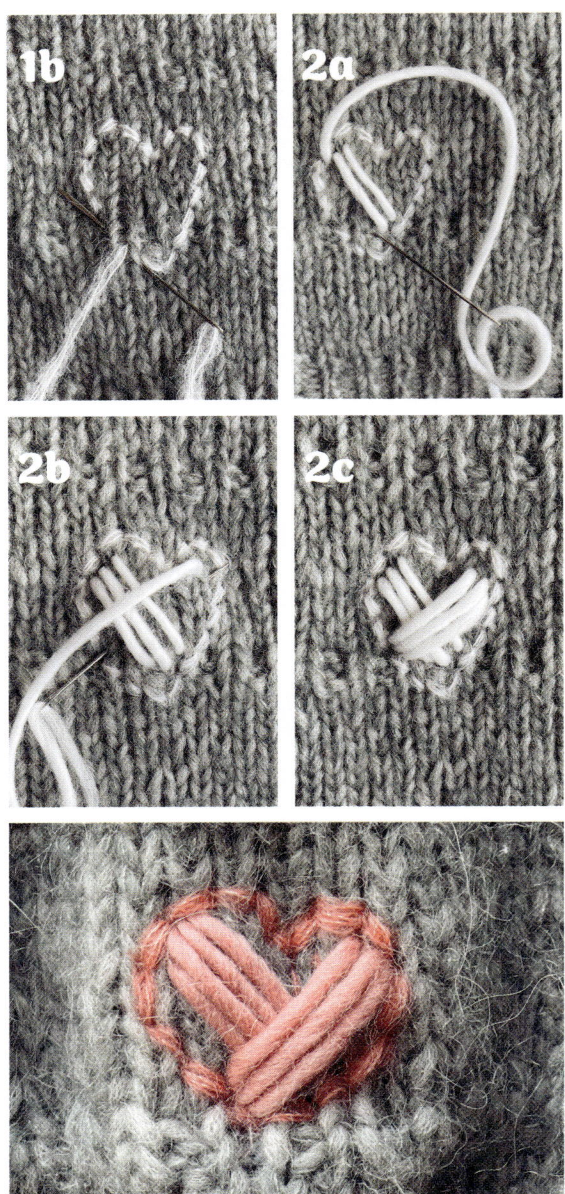

EMBROIDERY MOTIF AND WORKING DIAGRAMS

(shown at actual size)

DO SHARE YOUR EMBROIDERY ON INSTAGRAM USING THE HASHTAG: #LOUGHEARTTOHEART

Good Morning

These lovely eight-petalled flowers look stunning on a fluffy knitted background. In the sample opposite, the flowers are spread over the body and sleeves. Each flower is embroidered using three shades of red, in two different weights of yarn.

Embroidery techniques

- Straight stitch
- Satin stitch
- Lazy daisy (detached chain) stitch

Notions

- Two long, thin, sharp yarn needles – one for thin yarn and one for thick
- Scissors
- Stitch markers
- Embroidery frame (optional)

Yarn

Sandnes Garn: Kos (62% alpaca, 29% nylon, 9% wool; chunky / bulky / weight 5; 50g / 150m / 164yd)

50g Wild Rose 4333 (dusty rose pink)

50g Deep Burgundy 4372 (burgundy)

Sandnes Garn: Tynn Silk Mohair (57% mohair, 28% silk, 15% wool; 2-ply / lace / weight 0; 25g / 212m / 232yd)

25g Blossom 4213 (pink)

INSTRUCTIONS

Read through all the instructions before you start to embroider.

Each flower is composed of a centre star stitch surrounded by four large, symmetrical satin-stitched petals, finished with small lazy daisy (detached chain) stitched petals in between.

I placed my flowers randomly across the knit, but didn't put in too many as they're relatively large; however, for your own knit you can add more or fewer if you desire. I recommend marking out the positions of the flowers with stitch markers on the knitting, before you start to embroider.

Fasten off all the loose ends as you go. This will help to give your knitting a nice tidy back, and prevent your from inadvertently snagging previously worked stitches too.

1. Centre: With one strand of Kos in Deep Burgundy, embroider four straight stitches approx. 1cm / ½in long in a cross shape (**1a** and **1b**). Stitch two diagonal straight stitches over the cross to make a star shape (**1c**).

2. Petals: With one strand of Kos in Wild Rose, embroider five satin stitches that all start from the same point. Start close to the centre, bring the needle up from the back of the knitting, at the outer edge of the centre, and take it down again approx. 2cm / ¾in away from the centre (**2a** and **2b**). Bring the needle out at the same point you started until you have five layered stitches, giving your petal depth (see the diagrams and **2b**). To shape the petals further, add two more stitches either side of the layered stitches, grading the height of these stitches as shown in the photos and diagrams. Making the outer stitches shorter should give the petal more body and a prettier shape. Repeat for the right-hand petal (**2c** and **2d**) and for the bottom and left-hand petals.

3. Details: Using two strands of Tynn Silk Mohair in Blossom, embroider four lazy daisy (detached chain) stitches, one between each petal, placing them approx. 1cm / ½in out from the centre of the flower.

4. One flower made. Repeat until you have as many flowers as you desire.

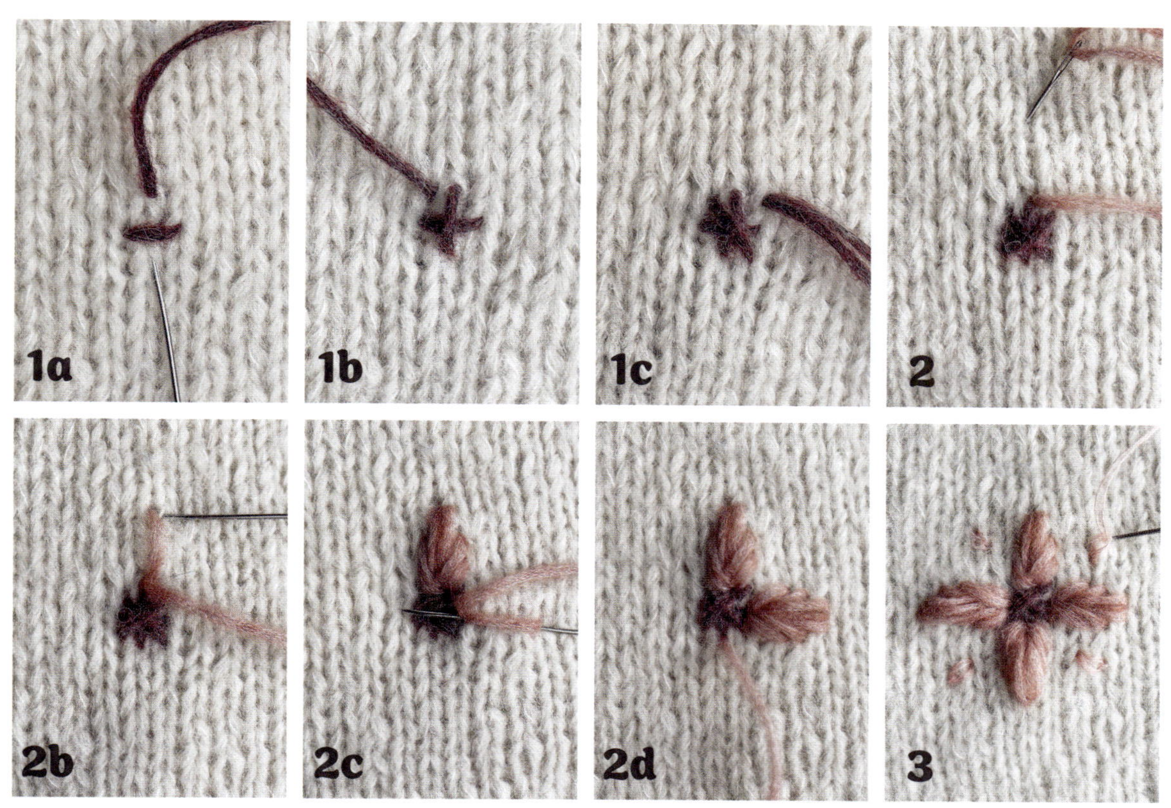
1a
1b
1c
2
2b
2c
2d
3

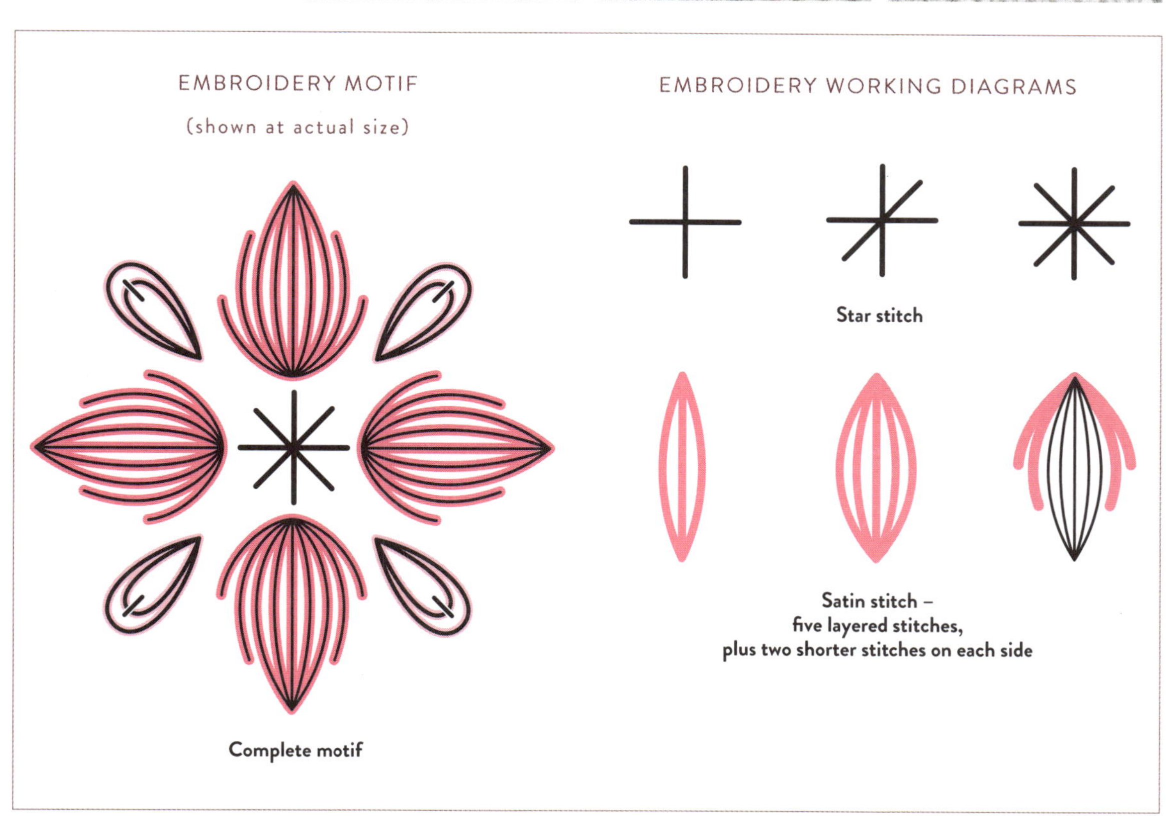
EMBROIDERY MOTIF
(shown at actual size)
Complete motif
EMBROIDERY WORKING DIAGRAMS
Star stitch
Satin stitch –
five layered stitches,
plus two shorter stitches on each side

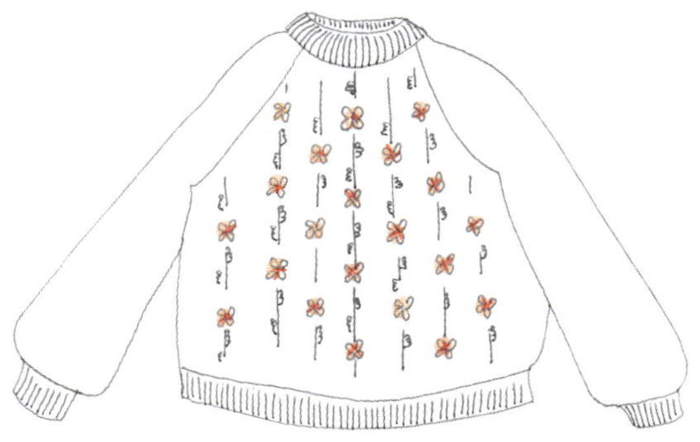

Pretty Flowers

This embroidery is made up of stalks of simple, four-petalled flowers, reminiscent of cherry blossoms. The design adds a delicate, feminine touch to any knitting, and would look wonderful on a sofa pillow cover as well as a sweater.

Embroidery techniques

- Chain stitch
- Lazy daisy (detached chain) stitch
- Straight stitch

Notions

- Long, thin, sharp yarn needle – use the thinnest, sharpest possible needle to make embroidering easier
- Scissors
- Stitch markers
- Embroidery frame (optional)

Yarn

Sandnes Garn: Tynn Silk Mohair (57% mohair, 28% silk, 15% wool; 2-ply / lace / weight 0; 25g / 212m / 232yd)

25g Deep Red 4236 (crimson)

25g Light Acorn 3041 (warm taupe)

25g Powder Pink 3511 (blush pink)

INSTRUCTIONS

Read through all the instructions before you start to embroider.

The main stalks are stitched with chain stitch, and run in parallel, vertical straight lines. There are seven stalks of flowers on the sample opposite, but you can embroider as many lines as you have room for on your knitting (although I'd recommend an odd number for a balanced design). There should be approx. 7cm / 2¾in between each stalk.

For each flower, embroider the petals with lazy daisy (detached chain) stitch, and then stitch a little cross over the centre. The small leaves are embroidered in the same colour as the stalks.

Always fasten off the ends as you go, to avoid catching and fraying the stitches on the wrong side of the knitting.

1. Stalk: To start the overall embroidery, create the long vertical stalks. Mark the stalks with tacking / basting stitches or a fabric marker. Begin with the stalk in the middle of the design then work outwards. Using two strands of Light Acorn, embroider each stalk in chain stitch, working from the top down. In the sample below, I worked from the bottom of the ribbed neckband down to the top edge of the ribbed bottom band; I also used a column of knit stitches as a guide, and embroidered each chain stitch in the middle of a knit stitch. You may need to adapt the design, depending on your own knitted base.

2. Flower: Mark where you'd like your flowers to be positioned on the stalks, with approx. 12cm / 4¾in between each flower. Try to stagger the flowers on alternate stalks, as seen in the photograph below left, to stop them looking too uniform. With two strands of Powder Pink, embroider four symmetrical petals for each flower. Each petal is made up of two lazy daisy (detached chain) stitches, one stitched on top of the other, to add volume. The petals should be approx. 1.5cm / ⅝in long.

3. Centre / cross: With two strands of Deep Red, embroider two diagonal straight stitches over the centre of the flower – over where the bottoms of the petals meet – to make a cross shape. The straight stitches should be approx. 1cm / ½in long.

4. Leaves: With lazy daisy (detached chain) stitch and using two strands of Light Acorn (I've used a slightly different colour in the steps and sample for clarity), embroider two groups of two or three leaves between the flowers – one group on the right side of the stalk, just below a flower, and the other group on the left side of the stalk a little farther down. The leaves should be approx. 0.5cm / ¼in long, and the second leaf of each group should be slightly longer than the leaves either side of it. Start and finish the stitching close to the stalk, and take care not to pull the stitches too tight, to avoid distorting and puckering the knitting underneath. If the stitches of your knit change direction, you have pulled the thread too tight.

DO SHARE YOUR EMBROIDERY ON INSTAGRAM USING THE HASHTAG: #LOUGPRETTYFLOWERS

1
2
3
4

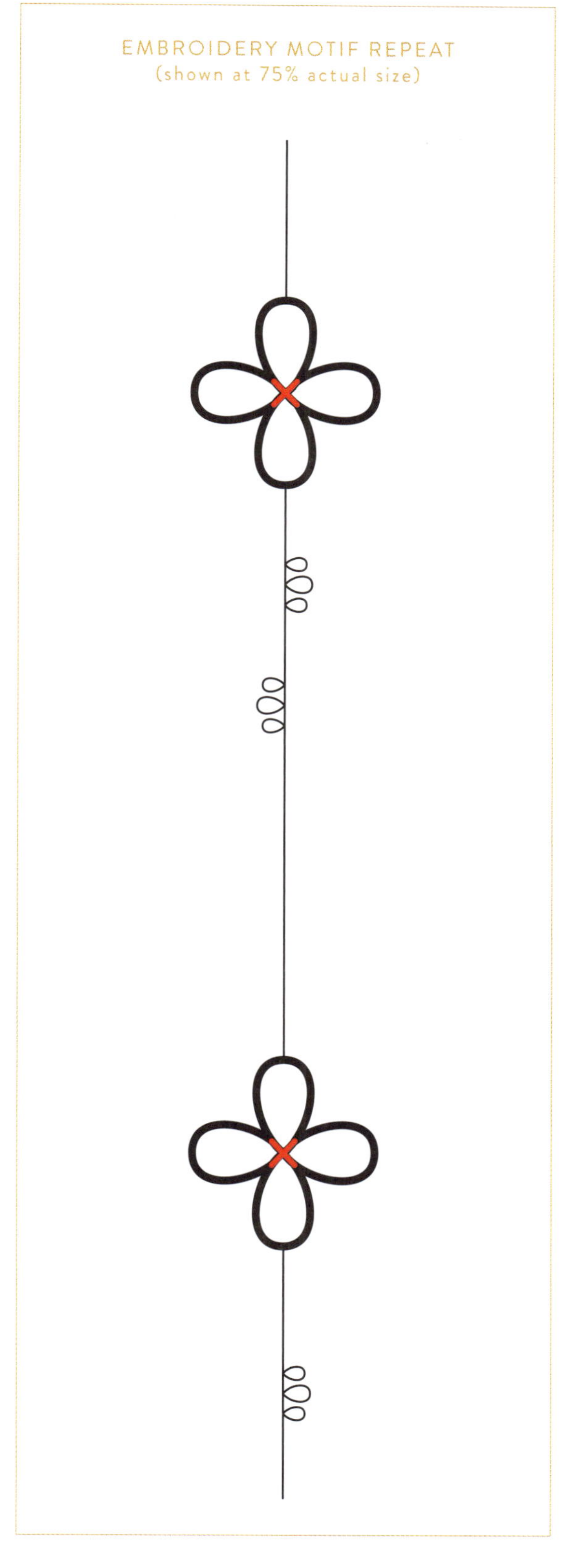
EMBROIDERY MOTIF REPEAT
(shown at 75% actual size)

Flower Power 2

These brightly coloured flowers will cheer up any knitted piece, and attract some deserved notice too! I've used mainly pink, red, orange and yellow shades, with touches of blue and green to add a bit of contrast. Feel free to use different colours, or what is in your own yarn stash.

Embroidery techniques

- Chain stitch
- Satin stitch
- French knots (optional)

Notions

- Long, thin, sharp yarn needle
- Scissors
- Embroidery frame (optional)
- Stitch markers

Yarn

HipKnitShop: Hip Mohair (80% mohair, 20% polyamide; lace / 2-ply / weight 0; 25g / 210m / 229½yd)

50g Berrylicious Red (cherry red)

50g Bubblegum Pink (bright pink)

50g In Love Pink (rose pink)

50g Candyfloss (pale pink)

50g Lemonade (pale yellow)

50g Here Comes The Sun (bright yellow)

50g Oh La La Orange (bright orange)

50g Jelly Bean Green (cool bright green)

50g Bubbly Blue (bright blue)

INSTRUCTIONS

Read through all the instructions before you start to embroider.

The flowers are embroidered randomly across the knitting in 13 colour combinations, using nine different shades of HipKnitShop: Hip Mohair. Note that only one of the colour combinations is described in the following steps; details on making flowers with the other yarn combinations used for the sample, along with photographs, can be found on pages 94 and 95. The making process is virtually the same for all.

The flowers are approx. 7–8cm / 2¾–3¼in in size. While you can make all the petals the same size, you can see from the examples on page 95 that fun results can be made when petals are different shapes. After marking your desired positions of the flowers with stitch markers, start by embroidering the centres of the flowers first then work outwards. Embroider one flower at a time. Fasten off all the ends as you go, to keep the back nice and tidy, and prevent snagging.

1. Start by placing a stitch markers across the knitting, each representing the centre of a flower. Avoid arranging the flowers in lines, and instead ensure there's a random yet balanced spread of them across the whole knitted piece.

2. Flower centre: Using two strands of your first colour, embroider a ring of chain stitches. The ring should be approx. 3cm / 1¼in in diameter.

3. Remove the stitch marker. With a second colour, embroider inside the ring with satin stitch. You have now completed the centre of the flower.

4. Petals: With two strands of the first colour, tack / baste the outlines of the petals, to use as a guide in the next step. The petals should be around 2.5cm / 1in long, but don't worry about making the petals uniform in shape and size: variety adds to the design, and gives the flower a very pretty, organic look.

5. One by one, fill the petals with satin stitch: divide the inside of each petal into three equal horizontal sections, then fill each row in turn with satin stitch (**5a**); this avoids too-long stitches, which are less secure. Start from the section closest to the centre of the petal and work outwards. Try to stagger the stitches between sections so each section overlaps another, to give you a smoother transition. Don't embroider too tightly; the stitches should lie flat beside each other. On the last outer section, embroider the satin stitches over the tacking / basting stitches so they are hidden.

6. Outlines: With the third colour, work chain stitch around the edge of each petal and around the flower centre. Take care not to pull the stitches too tight to avoid distorting the stitching and the knitting underneath.

7. Last of all, embroider another chain stitch outline around the centre of the flower, either in the same colour or a fourth colour.

8. Optional: To add texture, embroider French knots over the satin-stitch centre.

9. Repeat for the rest of the flowers.

DO SHARE YOUR EMBROIDERY ON INSTAGRAM USING THE HASHTAG: #LOUGFLOWERPOWER

EMBROIDERY MOTIF
(shown at actual size)

Here you can see pictures of all the flowers that are embroidered on my knitted sample. You can follow my suggestions, or make up your own variations based on what's in your yarn stash.

Flower no. 1

Centre: Berrylicious Red (cherry red)

Petals: Oh La La Orange (bright orange)

Outline: Bubblegum Pink (bright pink)

Flower no. 2

Centre: Jelly Bean Green (cool bright green)

Petals: Oh La La Orange (bright orange)

Outline: Berrylicious Red (cherry red)

Flower no. 3

Centre: Bubblegum Pink (bright pink)

Petals: Oh La La Orange (bright orange)

Outline: Berrylicious Red (cherry red)

Flower no. 4

Centre: Here Comes The Sun (bright yellow)

Petals: Lemonade (pale yellow)

Outline: In Love Pink (rose pink)

French knots:
Here Comes The Sun (bright yellow)

Flower no. 5

Centre: Bubbly Blue (bright blue)

Petals: Lemonade (pale yellow)

Outline: Jelly Bean Green (cool bright green)

Flower no. 6

Centre: Here Comes The Sun (bright yellow)

Petals: Candyfloss (pale pink)

Outline: In Love Pink (rose pink)

Flower no. 7

Centre: Bubbly Blue (bright blue)

Petals: Candyfloss (pale pink)

Outline: Berrylicious Red (cherry red)

Flower no. 8

Centre: Oh La La Orange (bright orange)

Petals: Candyfloss (pale pink)

Outline: Berrylicious Red (cherry red)

Flower no. 9

Centre: Oh La La Orange (bright orange)

Petals: Candyfloss (pale pink)

Outline: Lemonade (pale yellow)

Flower no. 10

Centre: Jelly Bean Green (cool bright green)

Petals: Bubblegum Pink (bright pink)

Outline: Oh La La Orange (bright orange)

Flower no. 11

Centre: Berrylicious Red (cherry red)

Petals: In Love Pink (rose pink)

Outline: Oh La La Orange (bright orange)

Flower no. 12

Centre: In Love Pink (rose pink)

Petals: Bubbly Blue (bright blue)

Outline: In Love Pink (rose pink)

French knots:
Here Comes The Sun (bright yellow)

Flower no. 13

Centre: In Love Pink (rose pink)

Petals: Jelly Bean Green (cool bright green)

Outline: Berrylicious Red (cherry red)

1
2
3
4
5
6
7
8
9
10
11
12
13

Strawberry Fields Forever

These large strawberries almost seem to pop out of the knitting! The strawberries are embroidered in thick yarn, giving them a bold, textured look. This design suits items knitted with large stitches.

Embroidery techniques

- Backstitch
- French knot
- Weaving

Notions

- Two long, thin, sharp yarn needles – one for thin yarn and one for thick
- Long, thin, blunt yarn needle, with an eye large enough for thick yarn
- Extra embroidery needle, for weaving
- Scissors
- Stitch markers
- Embroidery frame (optional)

Yarn

HipKnitShop: Fluff (80% kid mohair, 11% merino wool, 9% polyamide; chunky / bulky / weight 5; 50g / 100m / 109¼yd)

50g Berrylicious (cherry red)

HipKnitShop: Hip Wool (100% Peruvian Highland Wool; Aran / worsted / weight 4; 50g / 80m / 87½yd)

50g Coconut White (cream)

HipKnitShop: Wild Wool (38% alpaca, 37% Highland wool, 25% nylon; chunky / bulky / weight 5; 50g / 110m / 120yd)

50g Wild & Light Green (pale green)

INSTRUCTIONS

Read through all the instructions before you start to embroider.

Mark the positions of the strawberries before embroidering, ensuring there's an even spread across the whole knit. If you're adding strawberries to a garment, it's a good idea to try it on after this stage, to check you are happy with placements.

Each strawberry is composed of three elements: berry, seeds and calyx (the leafy section at the top). The berry is embroidered completely in backstitch – the outline is stitched first, then filled in with rings of backstitch. French knots represent the tiny seeds on the outside of the berry, and then the loose-hanging leaves at the top are worked using the weaving technique.

Fasten off all the loose ends as you go.

1. The strawberry: I recommend drawing the outline of each strawberry directly onto the knitting (**1a**). To make sure that the line of ink is covered by the embroidery, you'll stitch just outside the outline. Using a single strand of Fluff in Berrylicious, embroider the outline with backstitch (**1b**). Take care not to pull the stitches too tight (it's a good idea to use an embroidery frame to keep the underneath layer taut). Keep the stitches relatively short – one for every knit stitch you embroider over.

2. Working from the outline inwards, continue embroidering rings of backstitch inside the strawberry until you have filled it in.

3. Seeds: Using Hip Wool in Coconut White, embroider about six or seven three-wrap French knots randomly over the berry for the seeds.

4. Calyx: To embroider the leaves, you will need an extra embroidery needle. Note that the number of knit stitches you work into will depend on the knitted item. Insert the extra needle down into the middle of a knit stitch, from the right side and three knit stitches above the strawberry. Bring the extra needle up again at the very edge of the strawberry (**4a**). Thread the blunt yarn needle with one strand of Wild Wool in shade Wild & Light Green then bring it up from the wrong side of the knitting, to the right of where the extra needle exits the edge of the strawberry. Drop the needle, but don't fasten off. Wrap the yarn around the ends of the extra needle twice, in a counter-clockwise direction (**4b**).

5. Now weave the needle around the wraps – over, under, over from right to left for the first row; under, over, under from left to right for the second row (see the photograph '5' opposite); and so on. Weave as many rows as you can find room for. Try to avoid catching the needle in the actual knitting when weaving the leaf, so the leaves have a pretty, 3D effect. When the shape is filled, take the needle down to the wrong side of the knitting and fasten off.

6. Embroider two to three leaves for each strawberry in the same way. Varying the angle of the leaves (achieved by placing the extra needle in the knitting diagonally or even horizontally, rather than vertically) makes the embroidered leaves more lifelike.

DO SHARE YOUR EMBROIDERY ON INSTAGRAM USING THE HASHTAG: #LOUGSTRAWBERRYFIELDSFOREVER

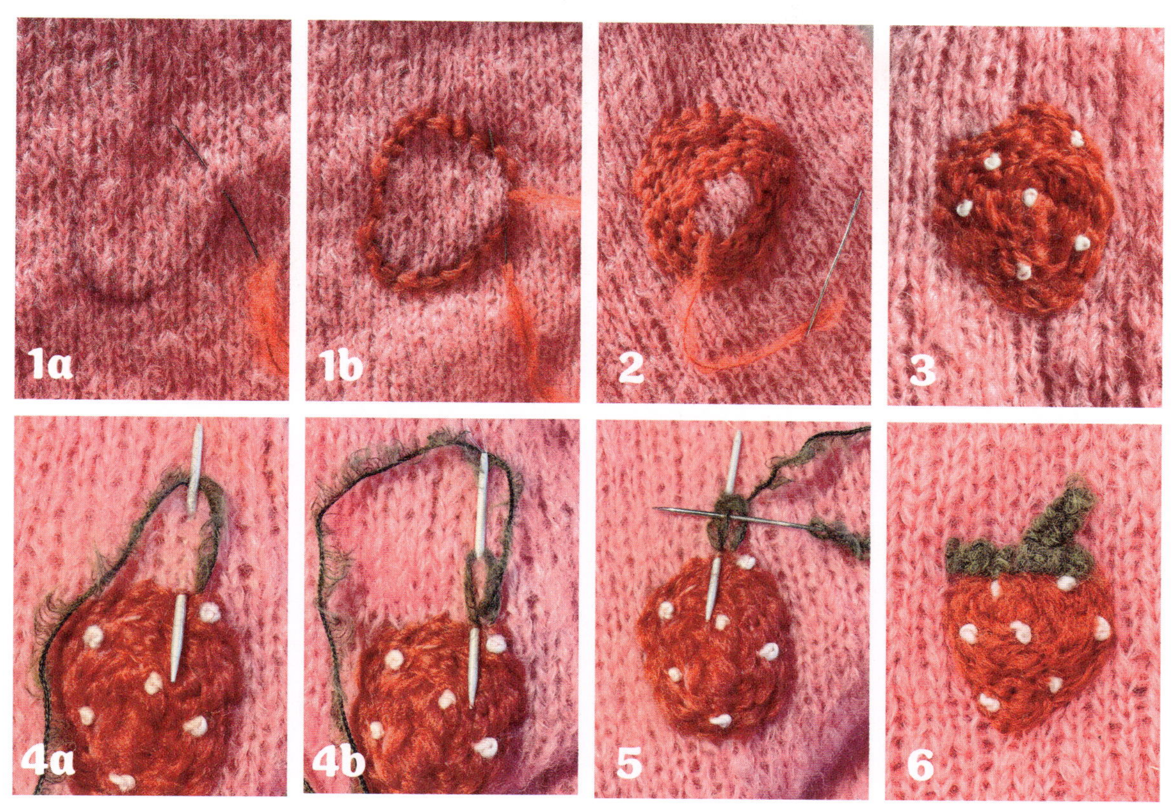

EMBROIDERY MOTIF
(shown at actual size)

Her Name Is Cherry

This gorgeous design features dangling, 3D cherries! To achieve this, the cherries and their stalks are made with crocheted chains and UK double crochet (US single crochet) stitches; the leaves are embroidered flat against the knitting with regular chain stitch. This design would look fantastic on a tote bag, purse or cardigan too.

Techniques

- Chain stitch (embroidered)
- Chain stitch (crocheted)
- UK double crochet (US single crochet) – UK dc (US sc)

Notions

- Long, thin, sharp yarn needle
- 5mm (US H-8, UK 6) crochet hook
- Scissors
- Stitch markers

Yarn

Sandnes Garn: Alpakka (100% alpaca; DK / light worsted / weight 3; 50g / 110m / 120yd)

50g Red 4219 (crimson)

Sandnes Garn: PetiteKnit Double Sunday (100% merino; DK / light worsted / weight 3; 50g / 108m / 118yd)

50g Statement Green 8236 (bright green)

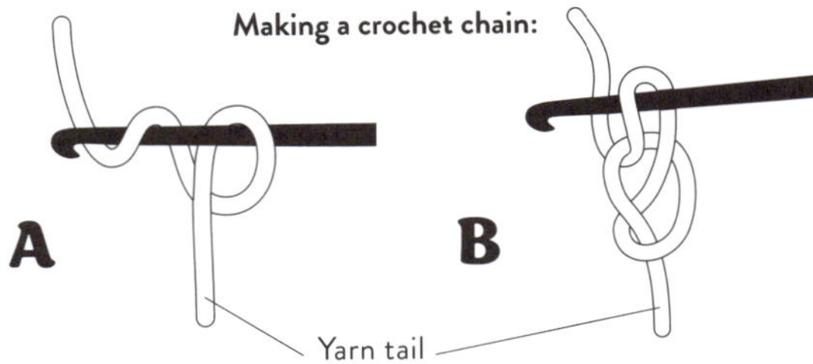

INSTRUCTIONS

Read through all the instructions before you start to embroider.

The crochet work in this pattern is easy, requiring only two kinds of stitches – chain stitch and UK double crochet (US single crochet) stitch. Each cherry is worked over eight rounds and then stuffed before the top is closed up to give the fruit a nice round shape. You can use up scraps of left-over red yarn for the stuffing. The stalks of the cherries consist only of a length of crocheted chain stitches. The leaves are made with embroidered chain stitch. The instructions below make a completed pair of cherries.

1. Cherry: Start by crocheting 6 chain stitches with two strands of Alpakka in Red: first make a slip knot, slide this onto the crochet hook, then make one chain with the working end of the yarn by following diagrams A and B above. Repeat the process shown in the diagrams five more times to make 6 chain stitches. Join the stitches into a ring by working 1 UK dc (1 US sc) into the first chain – twist the row of chains so you can insert the hook under the bottom loop of the first chain stitch, wrap the yarn around the hook counter-clockwise, pull the wrapped yarn through the loop back towards you (2 loops on hook), wrap the yarn around the hook counter-clockwise once more, then pull it through both loops on the hook. Place a stitch marker through the top V-shaped loops of this first UK dc (US sc) stitch to mark the start of the round.

2. Work another UK dc (US sc) stitch in the same chain stitch; this is an increase.

3. Work 2 UK dc (2 US sc) stitches in each of the five remaining chain stitches, increasing the stitch count to 12 stitches.

4. On the next round, you will work UK dc (US sc) stitches into both top loops (the V-shaped loops) of the previous round of UK double crochet (US single crochet) stitches. This time, you will increase in every alternate stitch as follows: *work 1 UK dc (1 US sc) in first stitch, work 2 UK dc (2 US sc) in next stitch*. Repeat from * to * to end of round = 18 stitches.

5. Work three rounds without increasing – 1 UK dc (1 US sc) in each stitch.

6. To decrease by 1 stitch, you work 2 stitches together (2tog). To work a UK dc2tog (US sc2tog) = insert the hook into the next stitch, wrap the yarn around hook counter-clockwise, pull through loop – 2 loops on hook, insert the hook into the following stitch, wrap the yarn around the hook counter-clockwise, pull through loop – 3 loops on hook, wrap the yarn around the hook counter-clockwise once more, pull through all 3 loops on hook. On the next round, decrease as follows: *work 1 UK dc (1 US sc) in next stitch, UK dc2tog (US sctog) in next stitch*. Repeat from * to * to end of round = 12 stitches.

7. On the next, final round, work 6 UK dc2tog (6 US sc2tog) = 6 stitches. Stuff the cherry with scraps of yarn, pushing them inside firmly with the help of the crochet hook. To finish, insert the hook into the first stitch of the round, wrap the yarn around hook counter-clockwise, pull the yarn through the stitch and the loop on the hook – this is process is known in crochet as a slip stitch. Crochet 1 chain then cut the yarn, leaving a 10cm / 4in tail. Thread the end tail into a needle then take it through a stitch at the top of the cherry and out of a stitch at the bottom of the cherry. Cut the excess yarn close to the cherry; the yarn tail should 'disappear' inside, on the wrong side of the cherry.

8. Make another cherry, following steps 1–7.

9. Stalk: Insert the crochet hook through a couple of stitches at the top of one cherry, pick up one strand of PetiteKnit Double Sunday in Statement Green then pull through (1 loop on hook), leaving a 10cm / 4in tail. Crochet a length of 20 chain stitches. Connect the end of the chain-stitch stalk to the top of other cherry with 1 UK dc (1 US sc). Then, crochet 1 chain, cut the yarn leaving a 10cm / 4in tail, and then pull the tail though the loop on your hook. Hide and cut away the excess yarn as for the cherry.

10. Assembling: Fasten the cherries to the right side of the knitting as shown opposite using a folder length of PetiteKnit Double Sunday in Statement Green.

11. Leaves: At the top of the stalks and using one strand of PetiteKnit Double Sunday in Statement Green, embroider the outlines of two leaves with chain stitch. Then, working from the outer edges inwards, fill in the leaves with rounds of chain stitch to finish.

EMBROIDERY MOTIF
(shown at actual size)

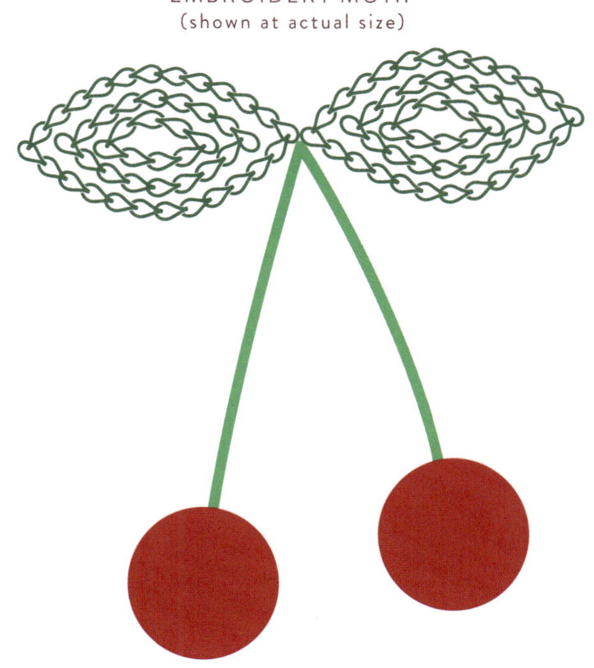

Poppin' Out

This 3D flower is made by combining embroidery and crochet. The petals are a mix of crocheted chain, UK double crochet (US single crochet) and UK treble crochet (US double crochet) stitches, which are worked around an embroidered centre.

Techniques

- Chain stitch (embroidered)
- Chain stitch (crocheted)
- UK double crochet (US single crochet) – UK dc (US sc)
- UK treble crochet (US double crochet) – UK tr (US dc)

Notions

- Long, thin, sharp yarn needle with an eye large enough for thick yarn
- 5mm (US H-8, UK 6) crochet hook
- Scissors
- Stitch markers

Yarn

HipKnitShop: Fluff (80% kid mohair, 11% merino wool, 9% polyamide; chunky / bulky / weight 5; 50g / 100m / 109¼yd)

50g Peach Cream (pale peach)

50g Baby Blues (light blue)

INSTRUCTIONS

Read through all the instructions before you start to embroider.

Each flower is made by embroidering a chain-stitch centre for the stamen; the petals are then made by initially crocheting arches of chain stitches, then working into the arches with UK double crochet (US single crochet) stitches, followed by UK treble crochet (US double crochet) stitches.

1. First mark the position of each flower on the knitting with a stitch marker, ensuring there is a nice, even spread. If you're embroidering a garment, I recommend trying it on after marking out the flower positions, before embroidering, to check that you are happy with the arrangement.

2. Flower centre: Start by embroidering a circular outline in chain stitch with one strand of Peach Cream yarn, the circle measuring approx. 3cm / 1¼in across. Embroider quite loosely, to avoid distorting the knitting – you can work in a spiral as you are going to be filling in the centre.

3. Working from the outside inwards, embroider rings of chain stitch one by one, or work in a spiral, to fill in the circle. Again, embroider loosely, and leave a tiny gap between each chain-stitch ring to avoid puckering the knitting underneath. Fasten off the loose ends on the back as you go.

4. Petals: You will start by creating the arches of chain stitches. With one strand of Fluff in Baby Blues, make a slip knot, slide this onto the hook, then insert the hook into one of the embroidered outer chains – do not insert into the knitting. Pull up a loop then crochet 1 UK dc (1 US sc) to secure (see step 1 on page 102 for instructions on how to work UK double crochet / US single crochet stitches), crochet 3 chains (see the diagrams on page 102 for instructions on how to crochet chains), then secure the end of the chain-stitch arch to an embroidered chain stitch, approx. two to three embroidered chain stitches along from where you started. Repeat to crochet a total of six arches around the outer edge of the flower centre, making sure the arches are evenly spaced. For the last arch, secure the end to the top of the first UK dc (US sc) stitch by inserting the hook into both top loops of the stitch, wrapping the yarn around the hook counter-clockwise, then pulling the yarn through the loop of the stitch as well as the first loop on the hook (this process is known as a crocheted slip stitch – sl st). Do not fasten off.

5. To fill in the arches, you will crochet around each chain-stitched arch. Do not work into the embroidered chain-stitched outline or knitting. To shape the petals, you will use a combination of UK double crochet (US single crochet) and UK treble crochet (US double crochet) stitches, as the two stitches have different heights. Work as follows: *around next arch work 1 UK dc (US sc), 3 UK tr (3 US dc) around same arch, 1 UK dc (1 US sc) around same arch; repeat from * for the remaining five arches. To finish, crochet 1 chain, cut the yarn leaving a 10cm / 4in tail, and then pull the tail though the loop on your hook. Weave in the tail of yarn on the wrong side of the knit.

6. Repeat steps 2–5 for the remaining flowers.

EMBROIDERY MOTIF AND WORKING DIAGRAMS
(shown at actual size)

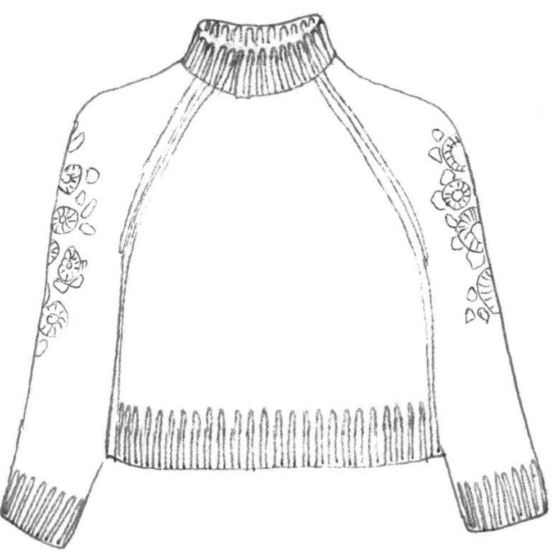

If You Believe

Embroidering in just one colour – even if it is the same colour as your knitted item – adds a surprising amount of impact. It creates a muted, sophisticated feel that is perfect if you're looking for a more classic look. For the sample opposite, the floral embroidery runs down the sleeves only.

Embroidery techniques

- Straight stitch
- Satin stitch
- Backstitch

Notions

- Long, thin, sharp yarn needle
- Scissors
- Embroidery frame

Yarn

Sandnes Garn: Alpakka (100% alpaca; DK / light worsted / weight 3; 50g / 110m / 120yd)

50g Natural 1012 (off-white)

INSTRUCTIONS

Read through all the instructions before you start to embroider.

The embroidery is simple and is made up of oval rings and leaves embroidered with simple satin stitches and straight stitches. The motif is narrow at the top and gradually increases in width around the centre, before narrowing again at the bottom. I recommend starting at the top and working downwards.

Fasten off all loose ends as you go for a nice, tidy wrong side.

EMBROIDERY MOTIF AND POSITIONING DIAGRAM
(shown at actual size)

1. Guide line: Start by tacking / basting a guide line in the middle of the area of knitting you wish to cover, working from bottom to top and using a contrasting colour (refer to the coloured dashed line on page 112). This guide line helps with the basic positioning of the embroidery.

2. Mark out the positions of the flowers with stitch markers around your guide line.

3. Flower: Around the stitch marker, draw a ring 2–4cm / ¾–1½in in diameter, depending on which flower you're creating from page 112. The ring doesn't have to be a perfect circle; a slightly irregular shape will look more organic. Over the drawn ring-shaped outline, and perpendicular to it, embroider 0.5–1cm / ¼–½in long straight stitches all around – work these like satin stitches but be careful not to overcrowd them. Work from the outside in and take care not to embroider too densely; the stitches should lie side by side, not on top of one another. The stitches will lie closer to one another towards the inside of the ring than at the outer edges, to give the appearance of the straight stitches radiating from the centre. It may help to rotate your work as you go. Fasten off the thread.

4. Repeat step 3 to embroider the rest of the flowers. Vary the size of the drawn circle, so you get flowers of different sizes. Work one flower at a time, and fasten off after embroidering each flower to keep the back of the knitting neat.

5. Small leaves: The small leaves are slightly triangular in shape, with the base close to the flower and the tip farthest away from it. They are made with vertical satin stitches placed side by side. Start by bringing the needle up from the wrong side of the knitting, out at the outer edge of the flower. Take the needle down approx. 2cm / ¾in away, at the tip of the leaf, then out close to the starting point but just to the left of it. Make a second satin stitch, taking the needle down at the leaf tip again and bringing it out close to the flower but slightly left of the previous stitch.

6. Repeat two to four more times, depending on the size of the leaf – taking the needle down at the leaf tip each time, but bringing the needle up slightly to the right of the previous stitch where the leaf meets the flower. Do the same to the right as well, until you have five to six satin stitches in total.

7. Long leaves: Embroider a line of backstitch approx. 3cm / 1¼in long (see the red oval stitches in **7a**). This is the centre line of the leaf. Fasten off. Fill each side of the backstitched centre line with satin stitches, working the satin stitches from the centre line outwards (**7a** and **7b**). The stitches should be approx. 1cm / ½in long, and point diagonally away from the centre line. Finish the leaf with two to three slightly shorter stitches at the top of the leaf (**7b**). Fasten off. Repeat for the rest of the leaves.

8. Leaves on stalks: Work curving lines in backstitch, using the diagram on page 112 as a guide for placement and size. These are the stalks. From these stalks, work small leaves in the same way described in step 5.

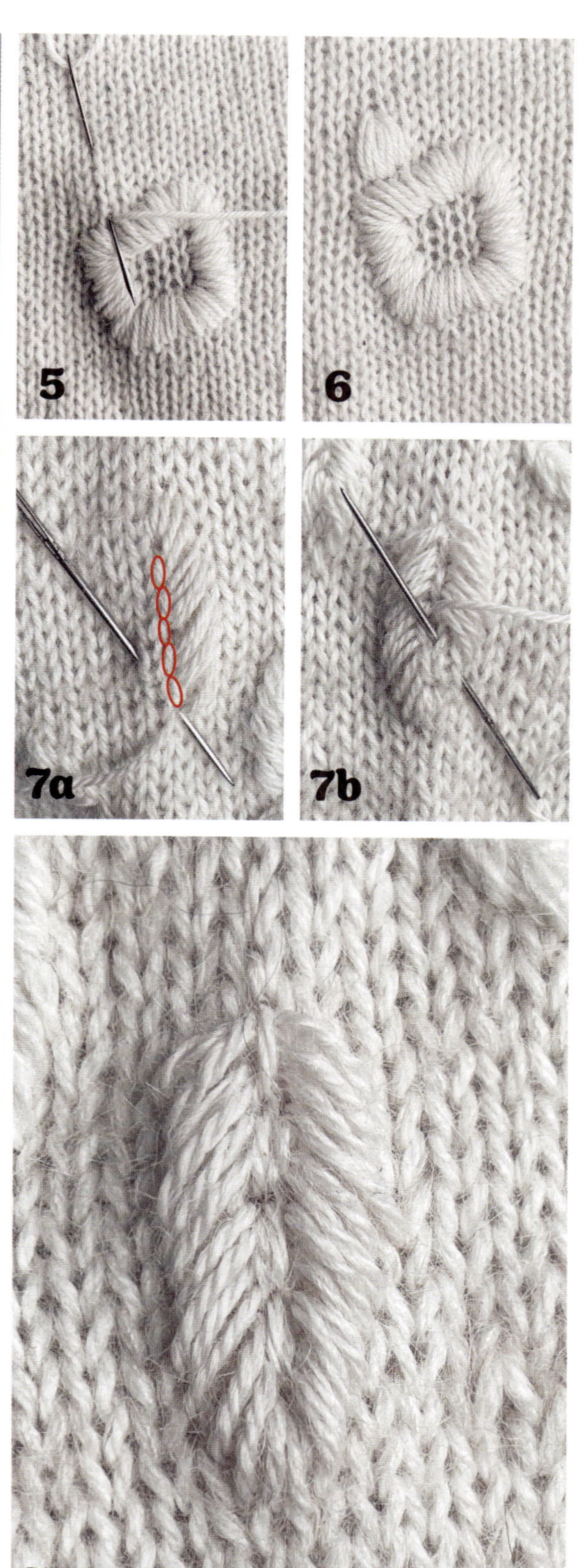

She's Got The Look

Decorate your knitting with colourful eyes! The sample opposite features seven different, finely detailed eyes, all worked in stranded embroidery cotton. For your own knit, you can choose to embroider all eyes, or just one of them.

Embroidery techniques

- Chain stitch
- Backstitch
- French knots
- Satin stitch

Notions

- Long, thin, sharp embroidery needle
- Scissors
- Stitch markers
- Embroidery frame (optional)

Embroidery thread / floss

DMC Mouliné Spécial
(100% mercerized stranded cotton thread)

B5200 Pearlescent White Light (white)

224 Earthworm (pale pink)

310 Metallic Black (black)

334 Light Indigo (blue)

444 Bright Yellow (yellow)

581 Grasshopper (green)

603 Macaroon Pink (hot pink)

728 Mustard (ochre)

738 Sahara (pale yellow)

740 Orange Papaya (orange)

762 Pearl Grey (grey-blue)

783 Old Gold (gold)

950 Beige (pale peach pink)

3790 Tree Bark (brown)

3841 Igloo Blue (light blue)

1

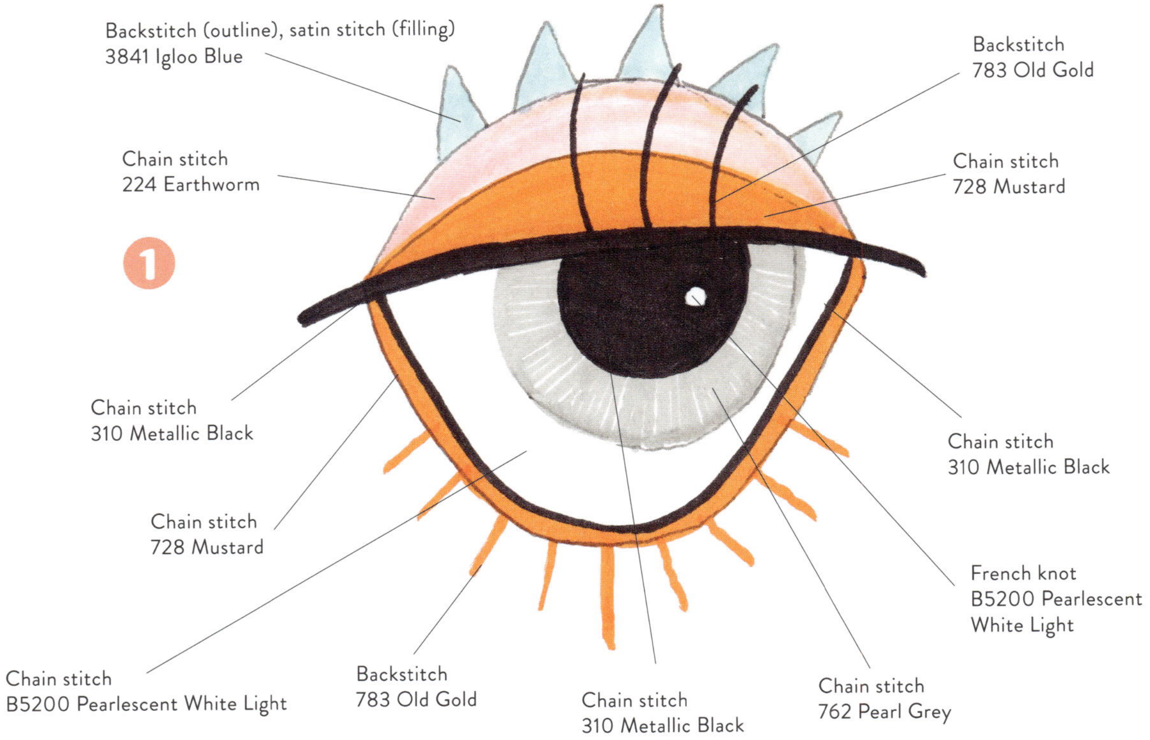

Backstitch (outline), satin stitch (filling)
3841 Igloo Blue

Backstitch
783 Old Gold

Chain stitch
224 Earthworm

Chain stitch
728 Mustard

Chain stitch
310 Metallic Black

Chain stitch
310 Metallic Black

Chain stitch
728 Mustard

French knot
B5200 Pearlescent
White Light

Chain stitch
B5200 Pearlescent White Light

Backstitch
783 Old Gold

Chain stitch
310 Metallic Black

Chain stitch
762 Pearl Grey

EMBROIDERY MOTIFS
(shown at actual size)

2

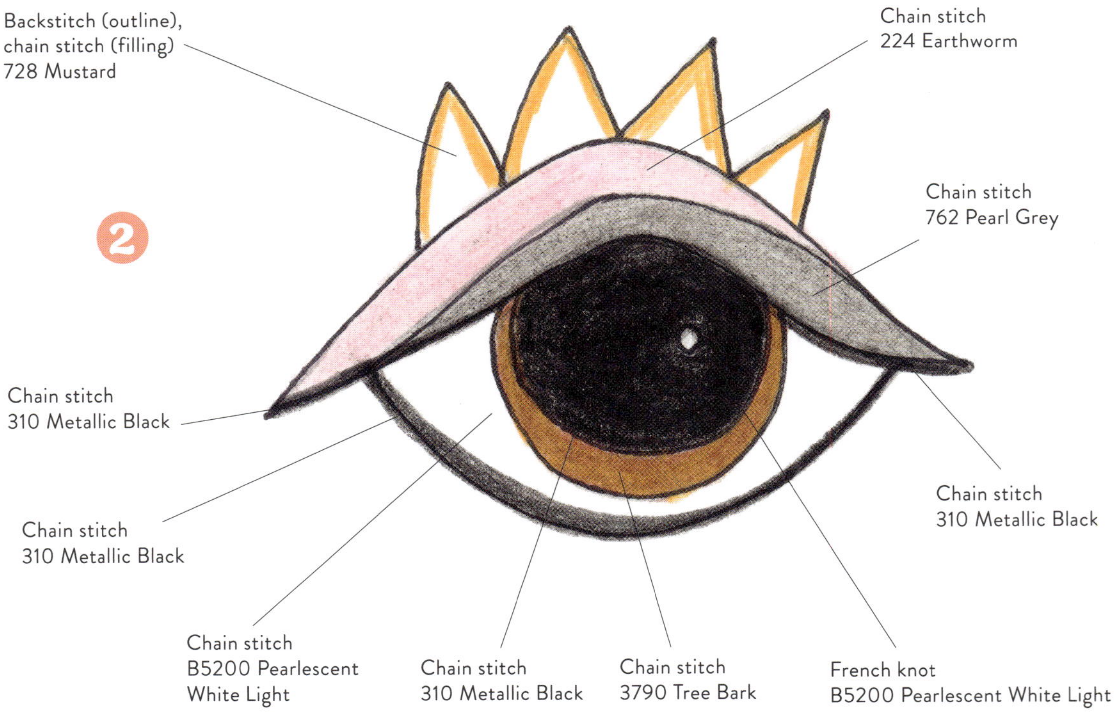

Backstitch (outline),
chain stitch (filling)
728 Mustard

Chain stitch
224 Earthworm

Chain stitch
762 Pearl Grey

Chain stitch
310 Metallic Black

Chain stitch
310 Metallic Black

Chain stitch
310 Metallic Black

Chain stitch
B5200 Pearlescent
White Light

Chain stitch
310 Metallic Black

Chain stitch
3790 Tree Bark

French knot
B5200 Pearlescent White Light

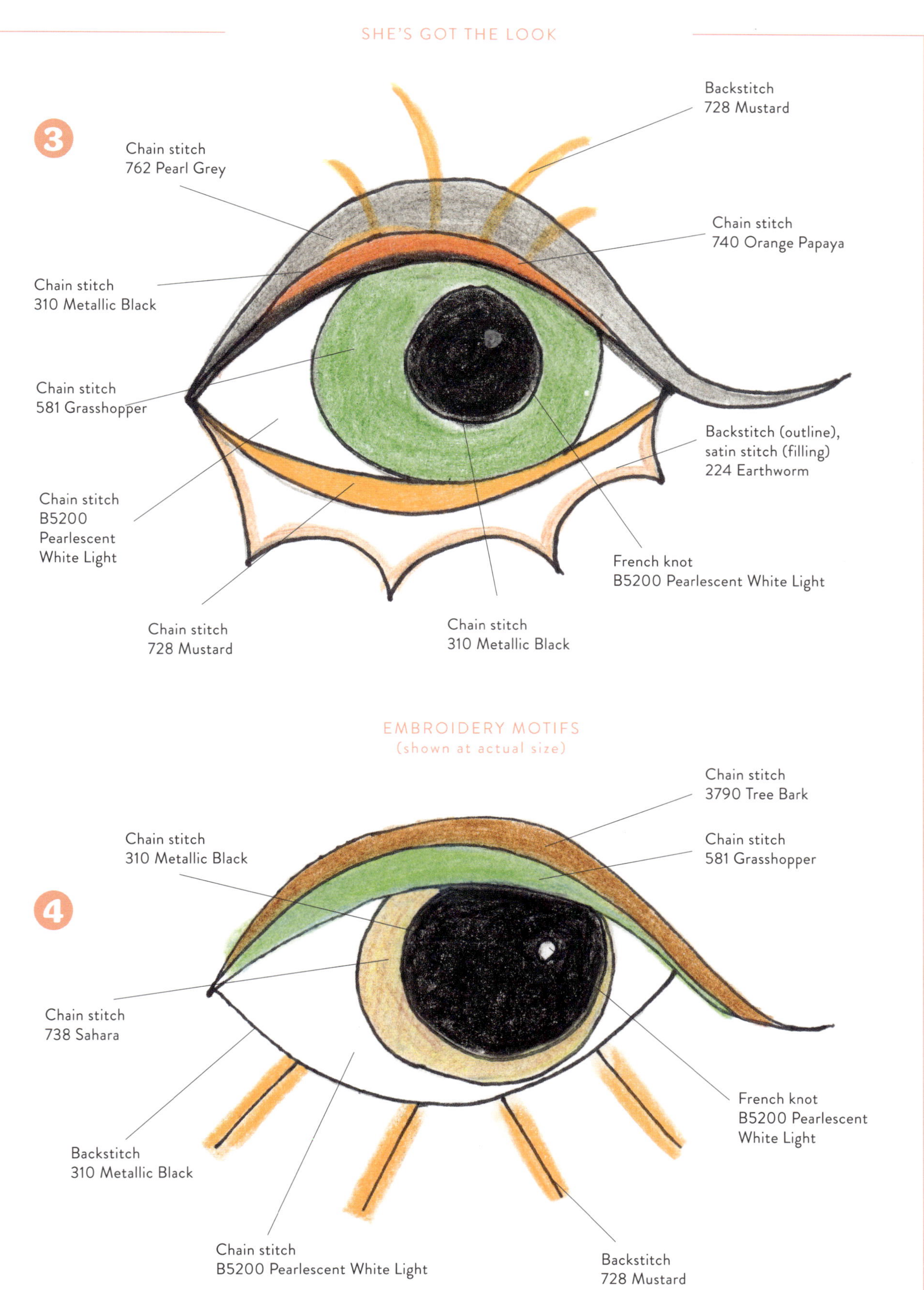

EMBROIDERY MOTIFS
(shown at actual size)

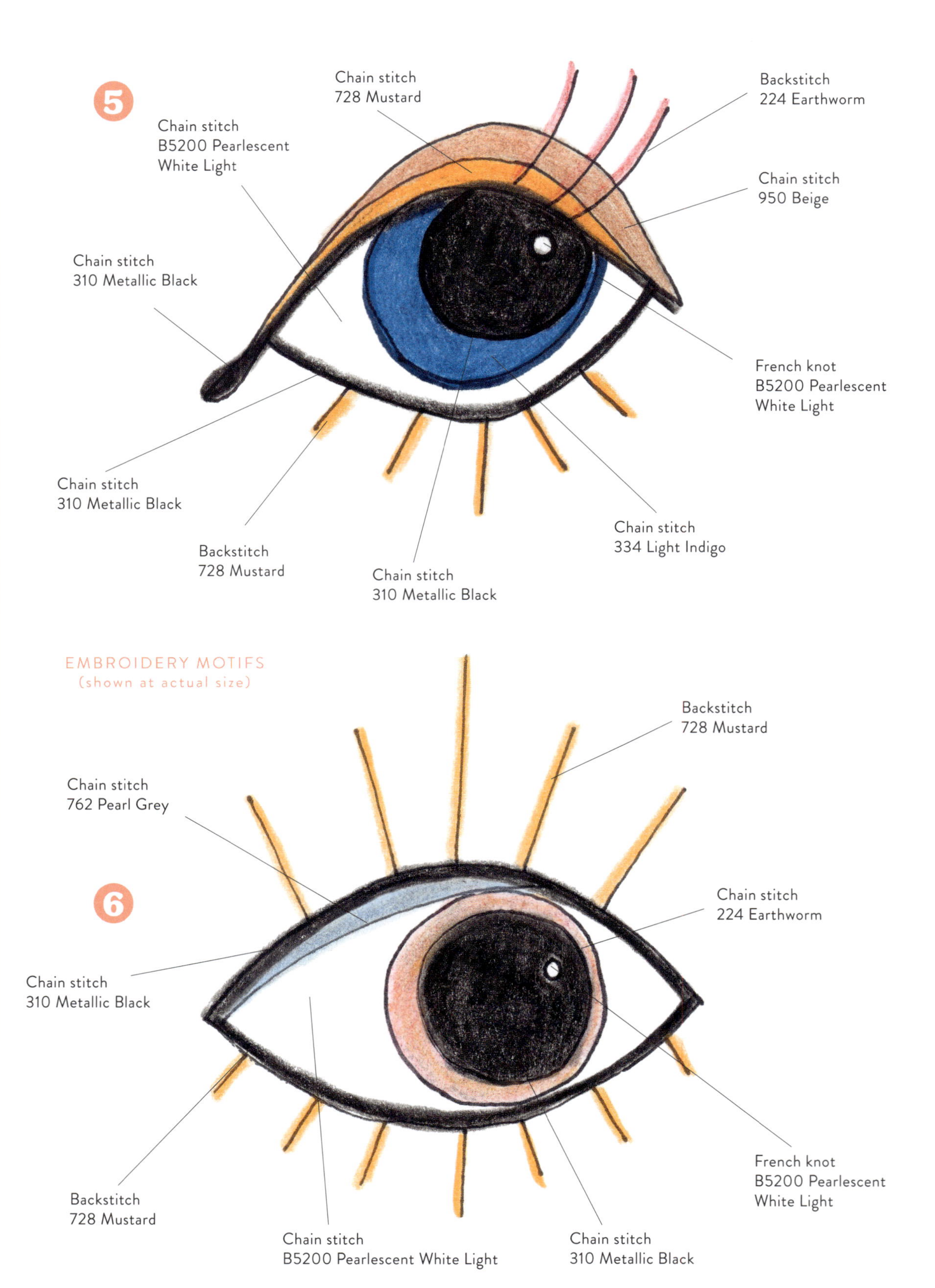
5
Chain stitch
728 Mustard
Backstitch
224 Earthworm
Chain stitch
B5200 Pearlescent
White Light
Chain stitch
950 Beige
Chain stitch
310 Metallic Black
French knot
B5200 Pearlescent
White Light
Chain stitch
310 Metallic Black
Chain stitch
334 Light Indigo
Backstitch
728 Mustard
Chain stitch
310 Metallic Black
EMBROIDERY MOTIFS
(shown at actual size)
Backstitch
728 Mustard
Chain stitch
762 Pearl Grey
Chain stitch
224 Earthworm
6
Chain stitch
310 Metallic Black
French knot
B5200 Pearlescent
White Light
Backstitch
728 Mustard
Chain stitch
B5200 Pearlescent White Light
Chain stitch
310 Metallic Black

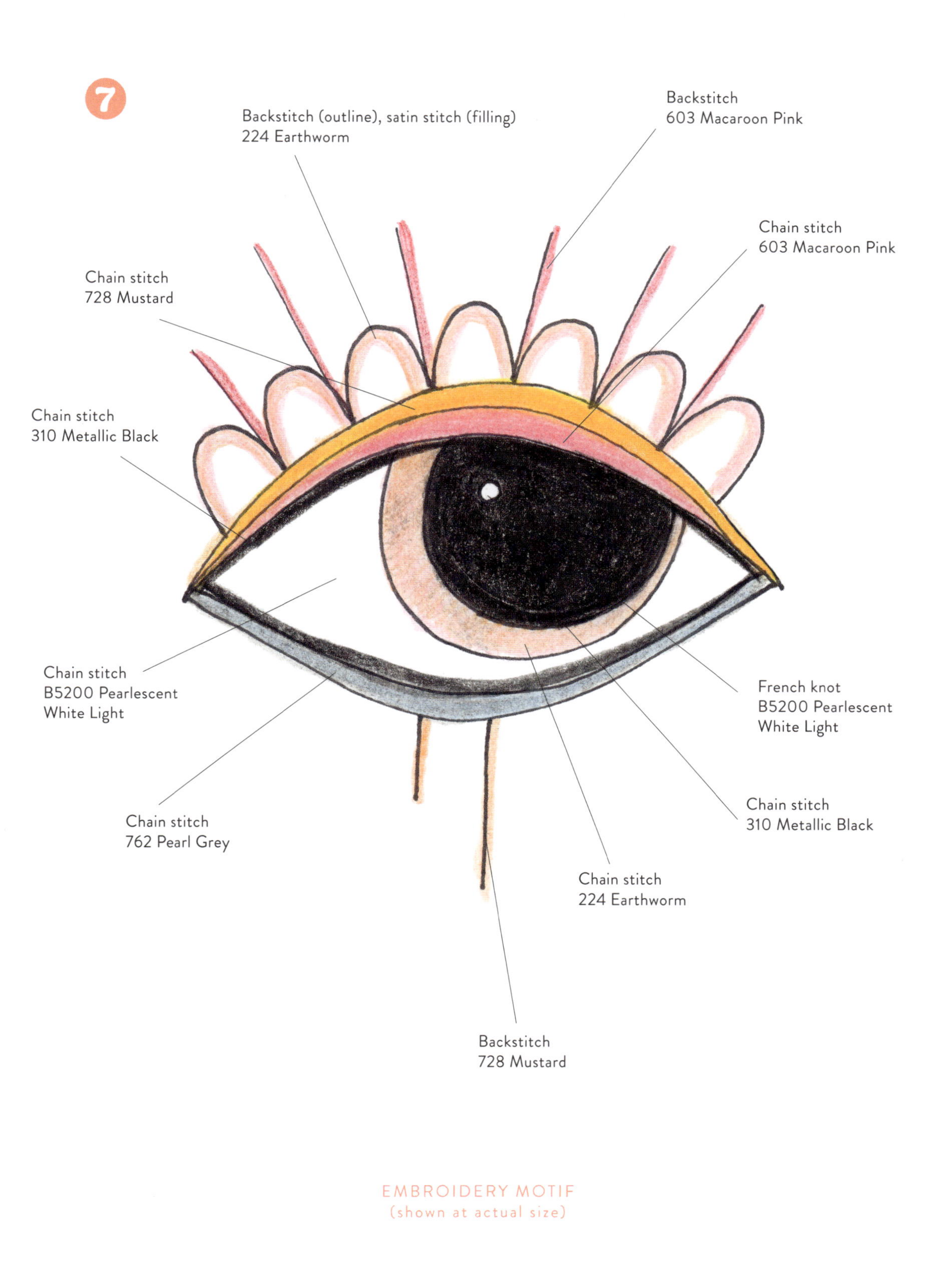

EMBROIDERY MOTIF
(shown at actual size)

INSTRUCTIONS

Read through all the instructions before you start to embroider.

For each eye, the embroidery cotton is split into two sets of three strands, to halve its thickness. Always start with the innermost part of the eye and work outwards. On pages 118–121, you can see illustrations of the eyes and the specific colours used. Fasten off each colour once you've finished with it, to keep the wrong side of the knitting neat.

Eye no. 1

(see diagram on page 118)

Colours: 3841 Igloo Blue, 224 Earthworm, 728 Mustard, 310 Metallic Black, 783 Old Gold, 762 Pearl Grey, B5200 Pearlescent White Light

1. Start by embroidering the bottom line of the upper eyelid in Metallic Black with chain stitch.

2. Pupil: Using chain stitch, embroider two-thirds of a circle in Metallic Black under the line of chain stitch (**2a**). From the outside inwards, fill the two-thirds circle with spiralling rounds of chain stitch, until the pupil is completely black (**2b**).

3. Iris: Using Pearl Grey, embroider two to three rings of chain stitch around the pupil. Start right next to the pupil and work your way outwards.

4. Upper eyelid: The upper eyelid has two parts – a bottom section (closest to the eyeball) and a top section. Start by embroidering the top part of the upper section in Earthworm with a curving line of chain stitch. Then, embroider parallel curving rows of chain stitch below this outline until you have covered half the overall eyelid. Change to Mustard and fill in the bottom of the eyelid with rows of chain stitch in the same way.

5. Lower-lash line: Embroider a curved line of chain stitch in Mustard approx. 1cm / ½in from the iris, which runs from the inner corner of the eye to just inside the outer corner of the eye. Inside this curve, backstitch a shorter curved line with Metallic Black, as shown.

6. Eyeball: Using Pearlescent White Light, fill in the area between the iris and the lower-lash edge with rings of chain stitch, working from the outside inwards.

7. 'Make-up' triangles: Using Igloo Blue throughout, embroider triangular outlines in backstitch, then in turn fill in each triangle with satin stitch.

8. Eyelashes: Using Old Gold, embroider three upper lashes and nine lower lashes in backstitch. (The upper lashes are black in the illustration for clarity.)

9. Highlight: Lastly, add a highlight to the black pupil with a French knot using Pearlescent White Light.

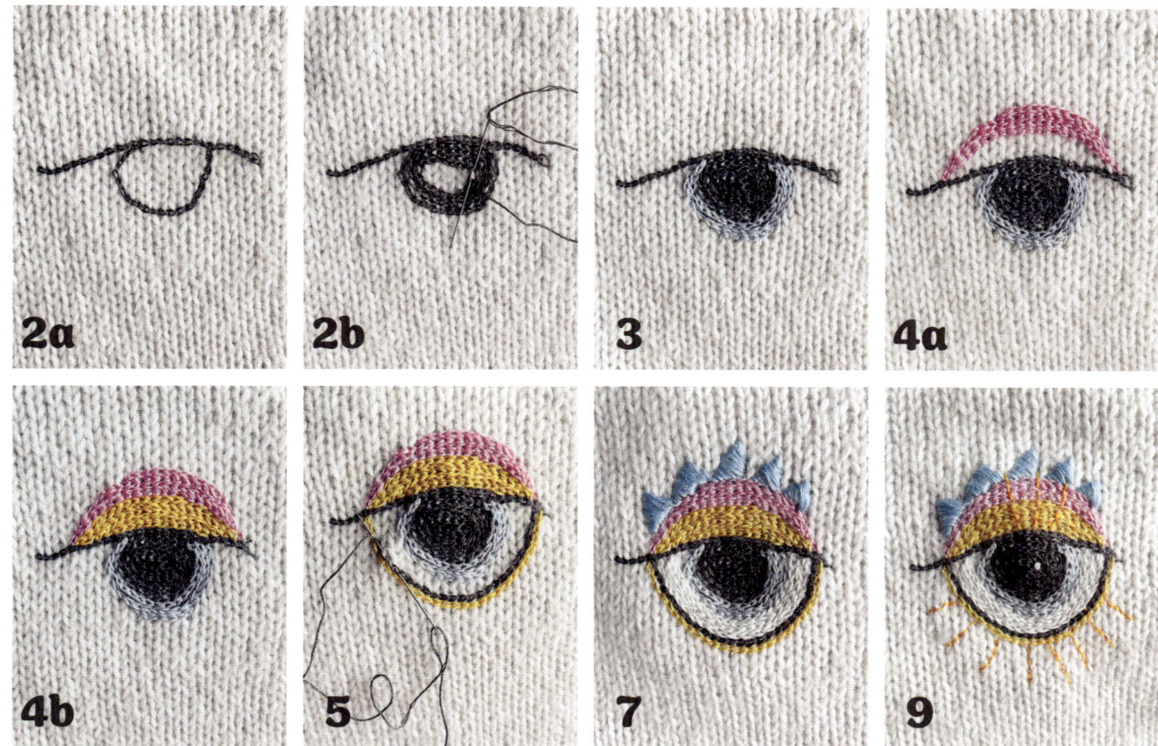

Eye no. 2

Colours: 728 Mustard, 224 Earthworm, 762 Pearl Grey, 310 Metallic Black, B5200 Pearlescent White Light, 3790 Tree Bark

Referring to the colours in the illustration on page 118, follow a similar process as described for Eye no. 1. This time, work only the top edges of the 'make-up' triangles with two to three rows of chain stitch in Mustard, and omit the eyelashes.

Eye no. 3

Colours: 762 Pearl Grey, 740 Orange Papaya, 310 Metallic Black, 581 Grasshopper, B5200 Pearlescent White Light, 728 Mustard, 224 Earthworm

Referring to the colours in the illustration on page 119, follow a similar process as described for Eye no. 1. This time, make the lower lash line thicker; omit the top 'make-up' triangles, and create a curvy, spiky 'make-up' shape below the lower lash line instead, and outline it with Earthworm; and stitch four upper lashes on the upper eyelid – don't stitch any bottom lashes.

Eye no. 4

Colours: 3790 Tree Bark, 581 Grasshopper, 738 Sahara, 310 Metallic Black, B5200 Pearlescent White Light, 728 Mustard

Referring to the colours in the illustration on page 119, follow a similar process as described for Eye no. 1. This time, don't add any stitching for the upper eyelid ('make-up' or upper lashes), don't stitch a lower lid (and you need just one row of chain stitch in Metallic Black for shaping the bottom of the eye), and embroider only four radiating lines of backstitches for the lower lashes.

Eye no. 5

Colours: 950 Beige, 728 Mustard, 310 Metallic Black, 334 Light Indigo, B5200 Pearlescent White Light, 224 Earthworm

Referring to the colours in the illustration on page 120, follow a similar process as described for Eye no. 1. This time, don't stitch any upper eyelid 'make-up'; you need just one row of chain stitch in Metallic Black for shaping the bottom of the eye, and embroider only three upper eyelashes and five lower lashes in backstitch.

Eye no. 6

Colours: 728 Mustard, 762 Pearl Grey, 224 Earthworm, 310 Metallic Black, B5200 Pearlescent White Light

Referring to the colours in the illustration on page 120, follow a similar process for stitching the eye as described for Eye no. 1. This time, stitch only the lower part of the upper eyelid in Pearl Grey, and create a thicker upper-lid outline in black with two rows of chain stitch; don't stitch a lower lid; don't stitch any 'make-up'; and embroider five upper and seven lower lashes.

Eye no. 7

Colours: 224 Earthworm, 728 Mustard, 603 Macaroon Pink, 310 Metallic Black, B5200 Pearlescent White Light, 762 Pearl Grey

Referring to the colours in the illustration on page 121, follow a similar process for stitching the eye as described for Eye no. 1. This time, stitch a scallop-shaped outline for the upper-lid 'make-up' with one row of chain stitch, then inside the outline fill in the upper edges in Macaroon Pink with two rows of chain stitch; stitch six upper lashes in Macaroon Pink and two lower lashes in Mustard.

See You

Each of these bold flowers has a beautiful, colourful eye at its centre, making a magical unique design. This garment will quickly become the jewel of your wardrobe.

Embroidery techniques

- Chain stitch
- Backstitch
- Satin stitch
- French knots

Notions

- Two long, thin, sharp needles – one for yarn and one for thread
- Long, thin, blunt yarn needle, for weaving
- Scissors
- Embroidery frame

Yarn

Note: This is used for the flower petals only.

Sandnes Garn: Alpakka
(100% alpaca; DK / light worsted / weight 3; 50g / 110m / 120yd)

50g Natural 1012 (off-white)

Embroidery thread / floss

Note: thread / floss is used for stitching the eyes.

DMC Mouliné Spécial
(100% mercerized stranded cotton thread)

B5200 Pearlescent White Light (white)

152 Old Pink (blush pink)

310 Metallic Black (black)

503 Thyme Green (eucalyptus green)

783 Old Gold (gold)

825 Metallic Gentian Blue (glaucous blue)

970 Neon Orange (bright orange)

992 Mint (bright mint green)

3766 Blue Green (turquoise)

3841 Igloo Blue (light blue)

FLOWER MOTIF – STITCH WITH YARN
(shown at actual size)

EYE MOTIF – STITCH WITH MOULINÉ THREAD
(shown at actual size)

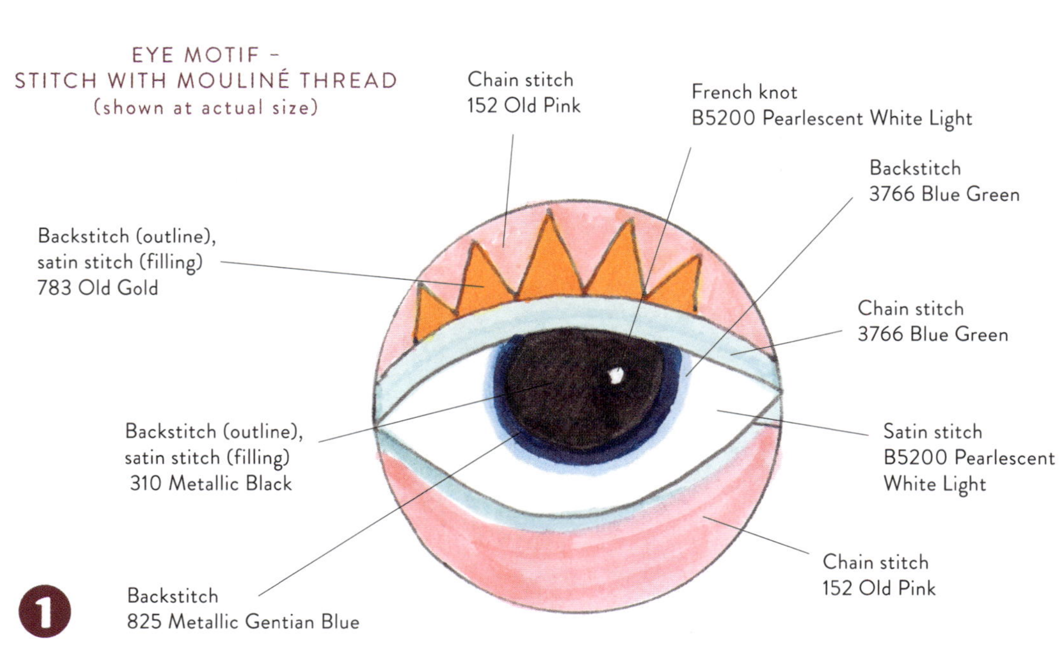

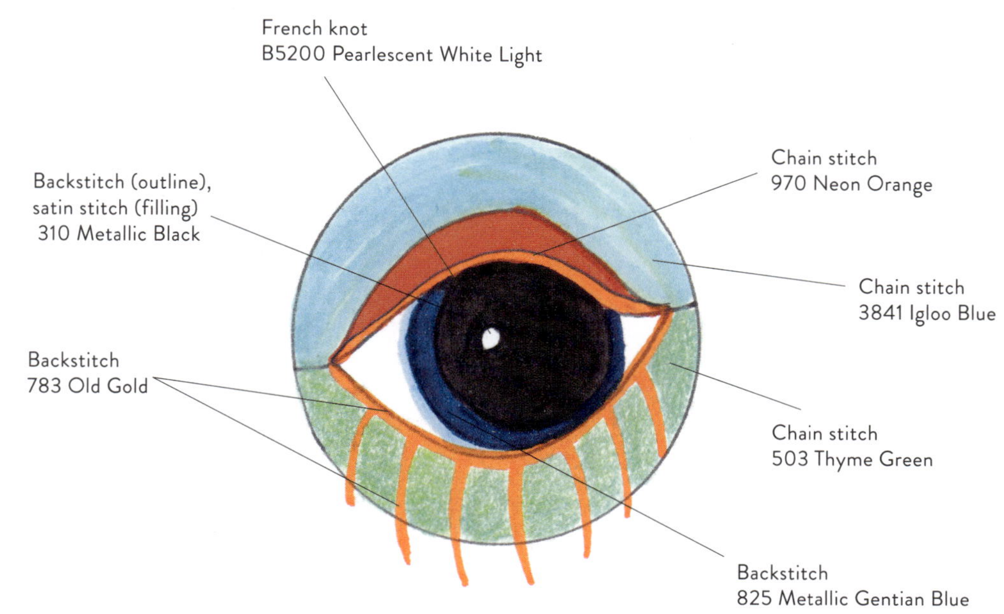

2

EYE MOTIFS – STITCH WITH MOULINÉ THREAD
(shown at actual size)

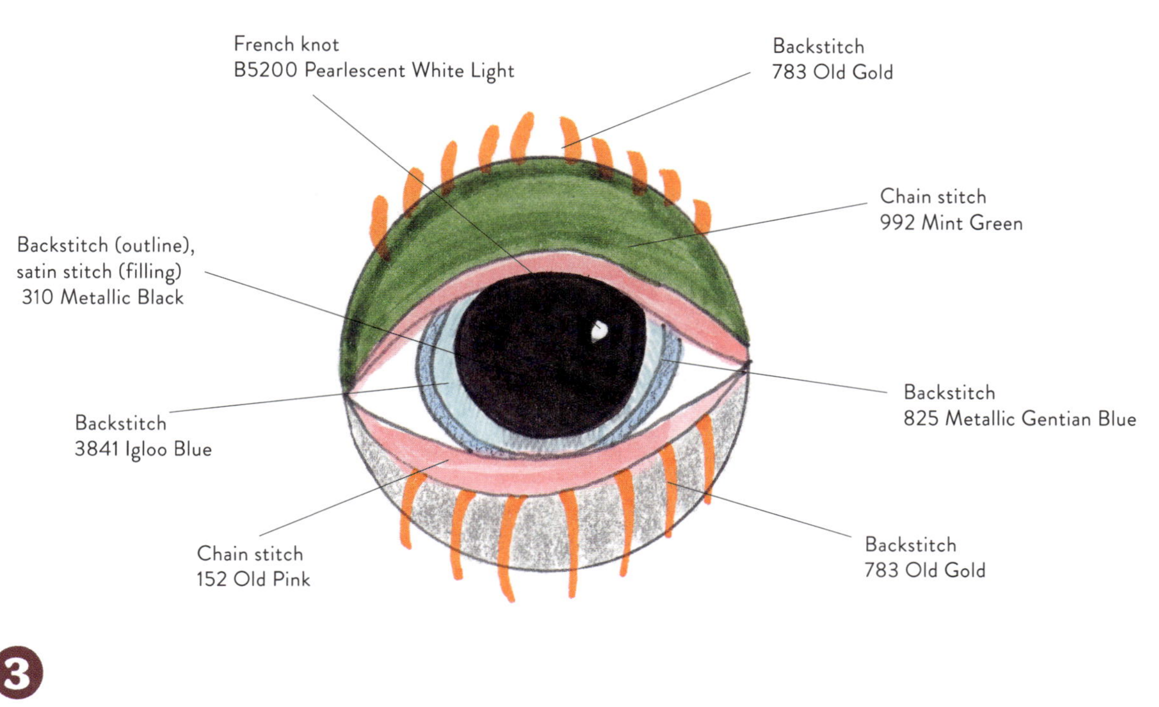

3

INSTRUCTIONS

Read through all the instructions before you start to embroider.

The eyes are embroidered first using Mouliné Spécial stranded cotton, then the petals are stitched around them with yarn. Combining different fibres creates an interesting contrast between the shiny embroidery floss and the coarser, matt yarn.

Use stitch markers to decide where to position your eyes on your knitting. Then, you can either use a transfer method to create guide lines to follow in stitch, or work freehand.

To stitch the eyes, you'll first split the floss into two sets of three strands, to halve the thickness. The outlines of the eyes are then worked in chain stitch, with backstitch used for the lashes. Please refer to pages 128 and 129, to see what colours are used for all three eyes. To stitch the petals, embroider the outlines in backstitch first before filling them in with satin stitch.

Fasten off the ends as you work, to keep the wrong side of the knitting tidy and to avoid snagging previous stitches.

DO SHARE YOUR EMBROIDERY ON INSTAGRAM USING THE HASHTAG: #LOUGSEEYOU

1. Eye shape: Embroider an approx. 5cm / 2in diameter circle with chain stitch using black floss. Each stitch should be approx. 2mm/ ⅛in long.

2. Inside the circle, and approx. 1.5cm / ⅝in down from the top of the circle, embroider an ellipse with chain stitch using the appropriate colour for the eye you are working – this defines the eye opening, and for Eye no. 2 it is worked in Old Gold.

3. Eyelids: Use chain stitch and black throughout. Above the top edge of the ellipse, embroider a curved line for the upper eyelid (the size varies from eye to eye; refer to the illustrations on pages 128 and 129), then embroider a line below the bottom edge of the ellipse for the lower eyelid if applicable. Note that the eyelids for Eye no. 2 don't extend to and touch the 'sides' of the circle.

4. Change to the relevant colour and fill in the eyelids with chain stitch as necessary.

5. Fill in the spaces between the eyelids and the black circle outline with rows of chain stitch. For this you need two colours, one for the upper half and one for the lower – refer to the relevant eye illustration on page 128 or 129. For Eye no. 2, where the eyelids are narrower, divide the spaces between the edge of the circle and each corner of the eye into two horizontal parts.

6. Pupil: At the centre of the eye, and ensuring it doesn't touch the bottom of the ellipse, embroider the outline of a three-quarter circle with backstitch using Metallic Black. Remember that the top of the pupil is hidden by the eyelid. Fill in the whole of the pupil with satin stitch, again using Metallic Black.

7. Eyeball: Fill the area around the pupil, and within the ellipse, with satin stitch using Pearlescent White Light.

8. Highlight: Embroider a French knot in the pupil, making it slightly off-centre, with Pearlescent White Light to create a highlight.

9. Iris: Embroider a row of backstitch around the outer edge of the pupil in your chosen eye colour, again remembering not to stitch around the top of the pupil, where it is covered by the upper eyelid. If you wish, you can add a second round of backstitch in another shade of blue (as shown in the diagrams for Eyes nos. 1 and 3) or even work multiple rounds of backstitch to make the iris more distinctive.

10. Lashes: Embroider the lashes in backstitch, working from the edge of the eyelid outwards. Each lash is made up of two to three short stitches, and you can choose how long you want them to be. Curve the lashes slightly, to make them more lifelike. For Eye no. 1, instead of lashes, outline the triangles above the upper lid with backstitch and fill with satin stitch using Old Gold.

11. Petals: Ensuring they're evenly spaced and using one strand of Alpakka yarn throughout, stitch nine to 14 petals around each eye (note that the diagram on page 128 shows the basic shape with 12 petals). Every petal should be approx. 3.5cm / 1¼in long, with the outlines stitched first in backstitch (the stitches of which measure 1–1.5cm / ½–⅝in long) then the insides filled completely with vertical satin stitches. To start stitch four petals – the middle-top and middle-bottom petals, then the middle-left and middle-right petals – to create a cross shape; then, fill each space between them with two more evenly-spaced petals. To fill each petal with satin stitch, I first divide it into three equal, horizontal sections then fill each section in turn with a row of vertical satin stitches, working from the base of the petal outwards. Ensure you stagger a few stitches between rows to merge them a little, as in the **7a** illustration on page 136. Start with the innermost section, then work outwards.

12. Petal outline (optional): Around each petal, backstitch an outline with three stands of Metallic Black.

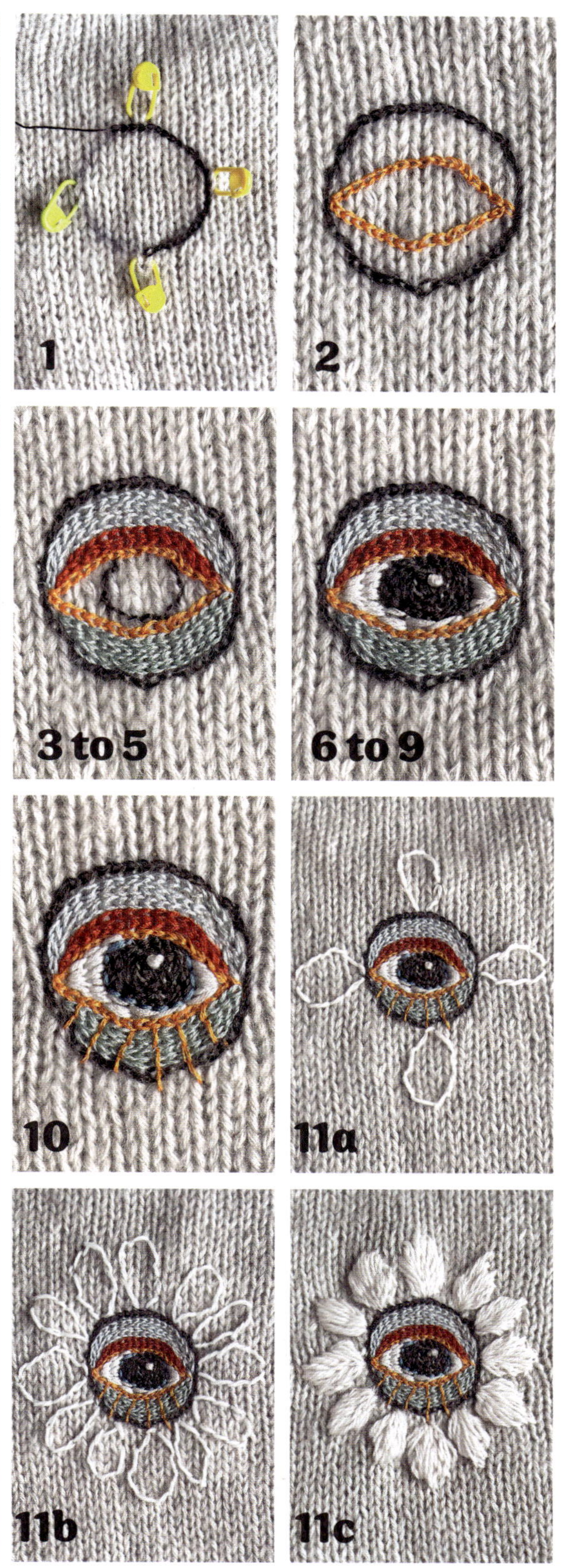

Made To Shine

These pretty, large flowers, reminiscent of magnolia blooms, look lovely in a meandering row across the chest of a garment, as seen opposite, but would be equally stunning stitched vertically at the ends of a scarf. In the sample opposite I've used a palette that echoes the colour of the knitted base that the flowers are embroidered on; however, you could use contrasting colours if that's your preference.

Embroidery techniques

- Weaving
- Chain stitch
- Satin stitch
- Backstitch
- Running stitch

Notions

- Long, thin, sharp yarn needle
- Scissors
- Stitch markers
- Embroidery frame (optional, but it can be very helpful to give you a taut and stable surface to embroider on, making it easier to avoid pulling the embroidery thread too tight)

Yarn

Sandnes Garn: Tynn Silk Mohair (57% mohair, 28% silk, 15% wool; 2-ply / lace / weight 0; 25g / 212m / 232yd)

25g Powder Pink 3511 (blush pink)

25g Light Acorn 3041 (warm taupe)

25g Blossom 4213 (pink)

25g Deep Red 4236 (crimson)

25g Jolly Blue 6046 (bright blue)

EMBROIDERY MOTIF
(shown at actual size)

INSTRUCTIONS

Read through all the instructions before you start to embroider.

I recommend using an embroidery frame if you aren't an experienced embroiderer, as the centres of the flowers are prone to puckering from all the stitching. Use two strands of Tynn Silk Mohair held together throughout. It's important to fasten off the ends every time you change thread; this will give your work a neat wrong side, and prevents any accidental snagging of previously worked stitches. Use the sharp needle for the majority of the embroidery stitches; switch to the blunt needle when weaving in step 3.

1. Before you begin, mark the positions of your flowers on the knitting. Place them in a row at slightly different heights for a more organic appearance. Remember that the flowers are approx. 9cm / 3½in in diameter, so you'll need to allow some space around each one.

2. Centre: Using backstitch and with Powder Pink embroider a circular outline measuring approx. 2cm / ¾in diameter.

3. Embroider six to seven parallel straight stitches across the ring (**3a** and **3b**). Note these should go over the outer edge of the ring. Take care not to pull the yarn too tight. If the knit stitches of the knitting twist in different directions, it means your embroidery is too tight. Now start weaving. You'll be working from one side to the other. Thread the yarn onto the blunt needle then take the needle over and under the horizontal straight stitches for the first column from one direction, then go under the stitches you went over and over the ones you went under for the second column in the opposite direction, then continue weaving in the same way for the third column in the original direction, and so on. Switch back to the sharp needle when done.

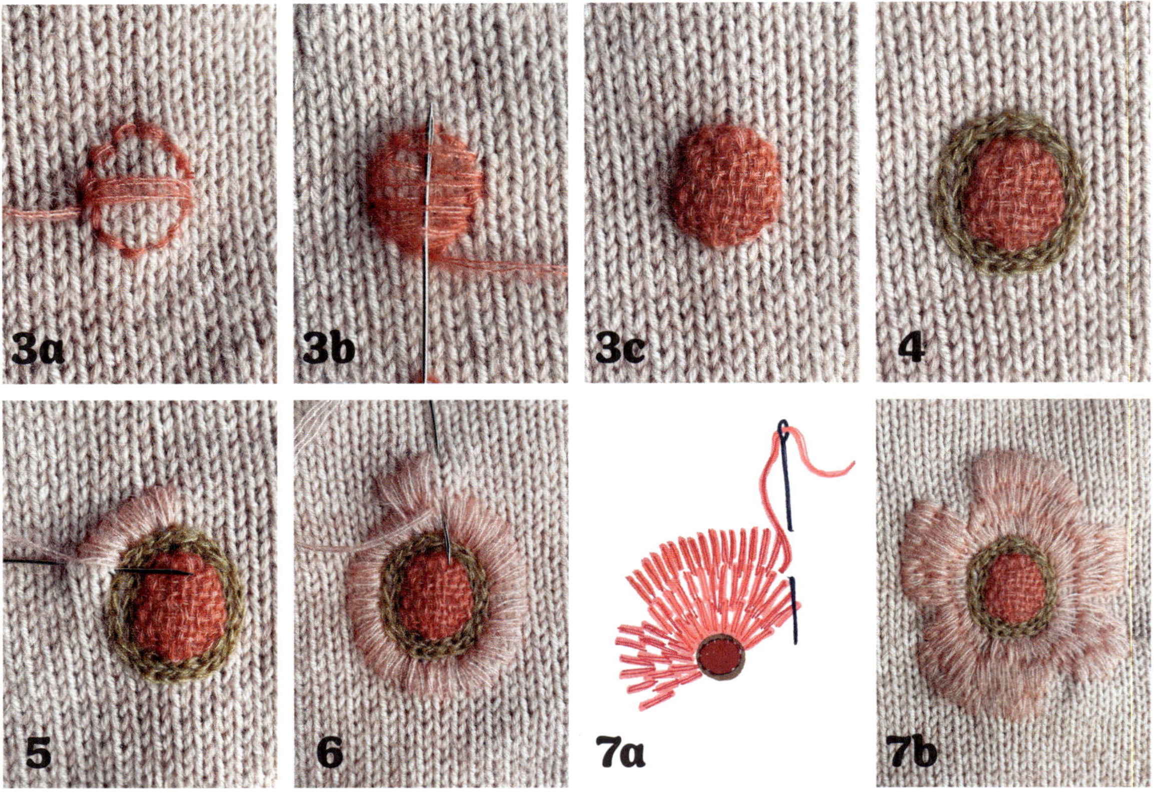

4. Ring around the centre: Embroider three rounds of chain stitch around the woven centre using Light Acorn.

5. Petals – area 1: The petals are built up with three rows of vertical satin stitches, with each row slightly overlapping the other rows to merge them a little. Start with the innermost area. Using Blossom, embroider vertical satin stitches around the whole flower centre, making the stitches approx. 1.5cm / ⅝in long and working from the outside in. Take care to keep the knitting smooth if you aren't using an embroidery frame. It is important not to embroider the stitches too close together – they should lie parallel with a little space between them.

6. Petals – area 2: Follow the same process above with the same colour, but this time leave five, evenly spaced gaps to begin shaping the petals. Remember to take the needle down between the stitches of area 1, to merge the two rounds slightly.

7. Petals – area 3: Follow the same process in steps 5 and 6 for the third and last area, but try to vary the length of the stitches a little so the shape of the petals look more organic and realistic. The petals are now complete.

8. Outlines: To give them a nice finish, embroider around the outer edges of the petals with backstitch using Deep Red. The stitches should be approx. 2mm / ⅛in long. Take care not to pull tight; it's better to make your stitches a bit loose.

9. Embroider running stitch around the outer edge of the flower centre using Jolly Blue, again making the stitches approx. 2mm / ⅛in long, to finish the flower. This produces a pretty dotted circle within the flower, reminiscent of the tiny round florets found at the centres of real flowers.

DO SHARE YOUR EMBROIDERY ON INSTAGRAM USING THE HASHTAG: #LOUGMADETOSHINE

Happy Little Things

This embroidery design is perfect for beginners, because the pretty little flowers are so easy to stitch. For the sample opposite, I embroidered the flowers in two colours.

Embroidery techniques

- Straight stitch
- French knots

Notions

- Long, thin, sharp yarn needle
- Scissors
- Stitch markers

Yarn

Sandnes Garn: Alpakka (100% alpaca; DK / light worsted / weight 3; 50g / 110m / 120yd)

25g Marzipan 2321 (cream-pink)

Sandnes Garn: Tynn Silk Mohair (57% mohair, 28% silk, 15% wool; 2-ply / lace / weight 0; 25g / 212m / 232yd)

25g Light Acorn 3041 (warm taupe)

INSTRUCTIONS

Read through all the instructions before you start to embroider.

The secret to the simplicity of this embroidery is its stylized appearance – each flower is made up of a delicate French knot centre with three straight-stitch petals, and each flower is about 2cm / ¾in in size, including the straight stitch 'leaves'. Embroideries don't come much easier!

Place stitch markers where you would like to position the flowers; for the sample opposite, I placed the flowers in slightly staggered rows, with the odd flower in a more random position for interest, and within the knitted centres of the columns of cablework.

Always fasten off the loose ends as you go; this will help to give you a nice tidy wrong side, and prevent you from snagging previously made stitches.

1. Petals: Using one strand of Alpakka in Marzipan, embroider three straight stitches for the petals – there is one stitch at the top that's perfectly vertical, and the other two stitches are at the bottom and diagonal; refer to the photograph and illustration, right. Start from the centre of the flower and work outwards, bringing the needle up from the wrong side of the knitting. Each stitch should be approx. 1cm / ½in long.

2. Leaves: Change to two strands of Tynn Silk Mohair in Light Acorn. In between the petals, embroider one straight stitch to represent the leaves. Make the stitches the same length as the petals.

3. Details: Finish the flower by embroidering a French knot in the centre, again using two strands of Tynn Silk Mohair in Light Acorn. Bring the needle up where the Marzipan straight stitches intersect, wind the doubled strands four times around the needle before taking it back down into the flower close to where the needle came up. Hold the loops in place with your finger as you pull the thread through to the wrong side.

4. Repeat for the other flowers.

EMBROIDERY MOTIF
(shown at actual size)

DO SHARE YOUR EMBROIDERY ON INSTAGRAM USING THE HASHTAG: #LOUGHAPPYLITTLETHINGS

Easy To Adore You

This cross and fringe design blends simple graphic motifs with texture. There are directions for embroidering crosses without the fringing too, in case you'd like to leave these out. The design works brillantly on the hems of garments, as seen in the sweater opposite, but would look fabulous at the bottom of a knitted bag.

Embroidery techniques

- Straight stitch

Notions

- Long, thin, <u>blunt</u> yarn needle
- Scissors

Yarn

Sandnes Garn: Alpakka Ull (65% alpaca, 35% wool; aran / worsted / weight 4; 50g / 100m / 109yd)

50g Coke Melange 1088 (heathered charcoal black)

INSTRUCTIONS

Read through all the instructions before you start to embroider.

I've given instructions for two kinds of motifs – one with fringing and one without. The motif with fringes has a stacked pair of crosses, one on top of the other, and the fringes are actually hanging yarn ends. The other cross motif is a simple embroidered row of crosses, as shown on the sleeves of the sweater and the hat opposite. Use two strands of Alpakka Ull held together throughout.

1. Crosses with fringes: In my sample, each cross extends roughly over six rows of stocking / stockinette stitch and four knit stitches – this will likely need to change for your own knitting. Start at the bottom-left corner of the cross. Bring the threaded needle up from the wrong side, at the cast-on edge (**A**). Take the needle down diagonally, approx. three knit stitches to the right and approx. five knit stitches up (**B**). Pull the thread through until it lies straight in a diagonal line.

2. Bring the needle up five stitches below where you inserted it last (**C**). Take the needle down diagonally once again, this time three stitches to the left and five knit stitches up (**D**). Pull tight.

3. Complete the cross by sewing a tiny vertical straight stitch over the point where the threads cross, locking the cross in place: bring the needle up from the wrong side above the intersection (**E**) then take the needle down below it (**F**) and pull the thread tight.

4. Finish by fastening off the thread and leaving about 10cm / 4in of thread hanging at the back after step 3 of the cross, creating a fringe.

5. Repeating steps 1–3 to embroider a second cross above the first one.

6. Repeat steps 1–5 across the rest of the edge, spacing the double crosses as desired.

7. Crosses without fringes: Follow only steps 1–3 above, and repeat as desired, along the edge to be embroidered.

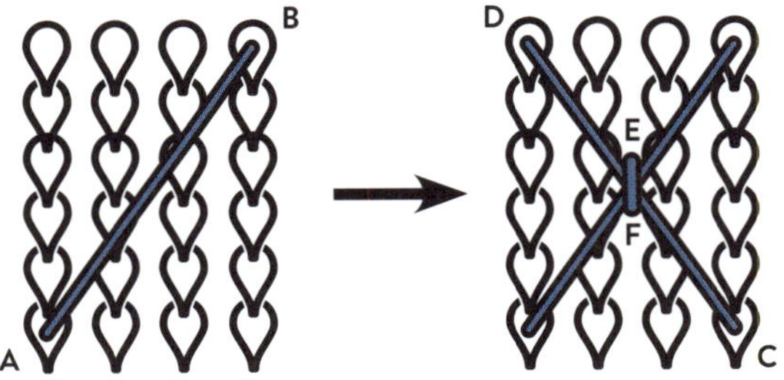

EMBROIDERY WORKING DIAGRAM
(not actual size)

DO SHARE YOUR EMBROIDERY ON INSTAGRAM USING THE HASHTAG: #LOUGEASYTOADOREYOU

Blue Flowers On The Sidewalk

These lovely little brunnera-like flowers look very pretty in a cluster over a large area, and add a simple, delicate layer of interest to any knitted piece.

Embroidery techniques

- Lazy daisy (detached chain) stitch
- Straight stitch
- French knot (optional)

Notions

- Long, thin, sharp yarn needle
- Scissors
- Stitch markers

Yarn

Sandnes Garn: Tynn Silk Mohair (57% mohair, 28% silk, 15% wool; 2-ply / lace / weight 0; 25g / 212m / 232yd)

25g Deep Blue 6081 (blueberry)

INSTRUCTIONS

Read through all the instructions before you start to embroider.

Each flower is embroidered with two strands of Tynn Silk Mohair held together. The flowers have five petals that all start from the centre of the flower. See the diagram on page 149 for the order of work.

Start by placing stitch markers where you want the flowers to be. If you're embroidering a garment, I recommend trying it on before stitching to check that you are happy with the positioning of the marked flowers.

Embroider one flower at a time, and fasten off after working each one, to keep the wrong side of the knitting neat and to prevent you from snagging previously worked stitches.

1. Petal outlines: Start by bringing the needle up from the wrong side of the knitting, at the centre of the flower.

2. From this point, embroider five lazy daisy (detached chain) stitches, referring to the working diagram opposite. Each lazy daisy (detached chain) stitch should be roughly 1.25cm / ½in long. The first lazy daisy (detached chain) stitch should lean to the bottom left, the second to the bottom right and the third should point straight up; the last two should be stitched in the spaces either side of this top straight stitch and point diagonally upwards.

3. Petal fills: Now fill in the petals with a single straight stitch. For each petal, start by bringing the needle at the centre of the flower, where the bases of the lazy-daisy petals intersect. Take the needle down at the tip of the petal then out at the centre again, ready to work the next stitch. Repeat for all five petals.

4. Adding a flower centre (optional): If desired, stitch a four-wrap French knot over the centre of the flower, over the bases of the petals.

5. Repeat steps 1–3 (or steps 1–4) until you have the desired number of flowers.

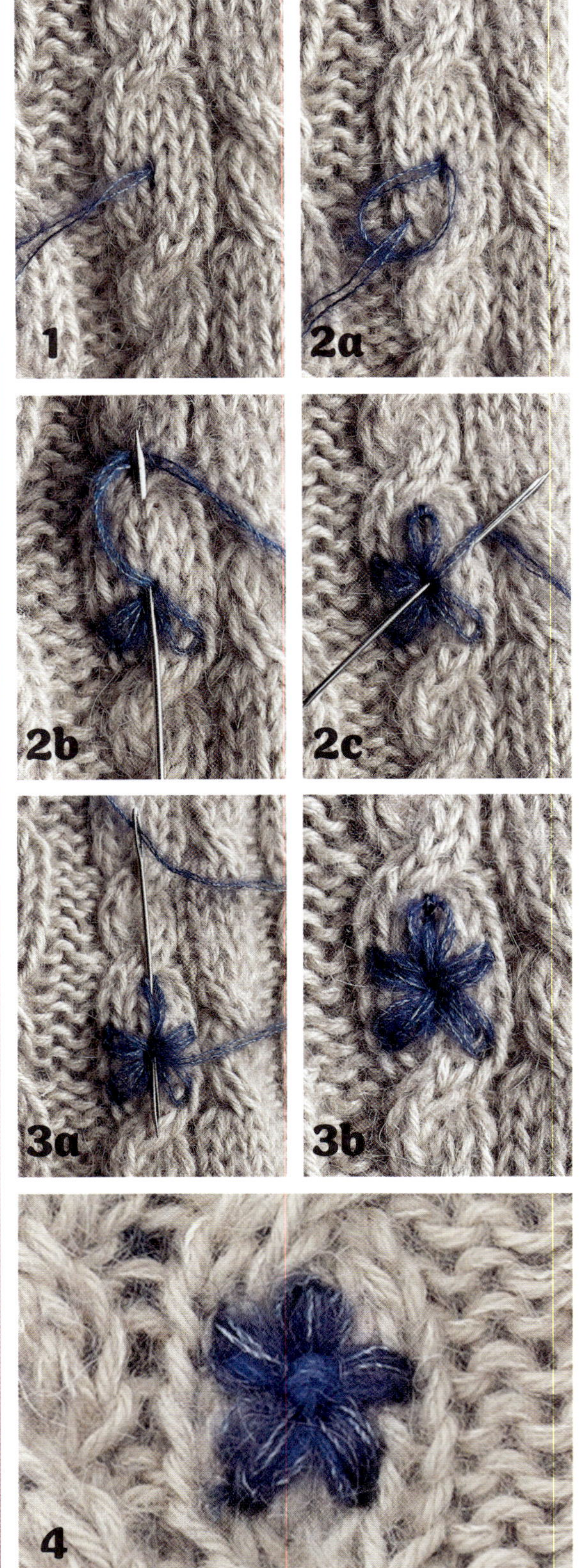

DO SHARE YOUR EMBROIDERY ON INSTAGRAM USING THE HASHTAG: #LOUGBLUEFLOWERSONTHESIDEWALK

EMBROIDERY MOTIF AND WORKING DIAGRAM
(shown at actual size)

Square

It's hip to be square! This bold, textured embroidery design consists of two rows of squares embroidered in duplicate stitch, with fun yarn tails at the corners for texture. The squares in the sample opposite are embroidered in 11 different colours, but feel free to use more or fewer shades, and in your own favourite colours. This is another design that's great for using up scraps of yarn.

Embroidery techniques

- Duplicate stitch

Notions

- Two long, thin, blunt yarn needles – one for thin yarn and one for thick
- Scissors

Yarn

HipKnitShop: Hip Wool (100% Peruvian Highland Wool; Aran / worsted / weight 4; 50g / 80m / 87½yd)

50g Hey Sailor (sea blue)

50g Falling For You Blue (bright blue)

50g Pale Blue (light blue)

50g Teddy Bear Brown (brown)

50g On Fire Orange (bright orange)

50g Dancing Snowflake White (off-white)

HipKnitShop: Hip Mohair (80% mohair, 20% polyamide; lace / 2-ply / weight 0; 25g / 210m / 229½yd)

25g Petrol Blue (petrol blue)

25g Hey Foxy Grey (silver grey)

25g Bubbly Blue (bright blue)

25g Cotton Ball White (pure white)

25g Oh La La Orange (bright orange)

INSTRUCTIONS

Read through all the instructions before you start to embroider.

Only duplicate stitch is used to embroider the squares. A square consists of four duplicate stitches in width and four rows of duplicate stitch in height. For my sample, as the knit stitches are small, each duplicate stitch covers two knit stitches in height.

I encourage you to mix the colours and yarns, and make as many variations as possible! Typically, you will use two strands of yarn held together – one of Hip Wool and one of Hip Mohair. It's possible to use only Hip Mohair; you will just need to hold together more strands of yarn to obtain about the same thickness. The squares will vary a little in size with the different yarn qualities, producing a more organic, hand-made look that I love.

I chose to keep the thread ends as fringes, but if you don't like that, fasten them off at the back at the end.

DO SHARE YOUR EMBROIDERY ON INSTAGRAM USING THE HASHTAG: #LOUGSQUARE

EMBROIDERY PATTERN

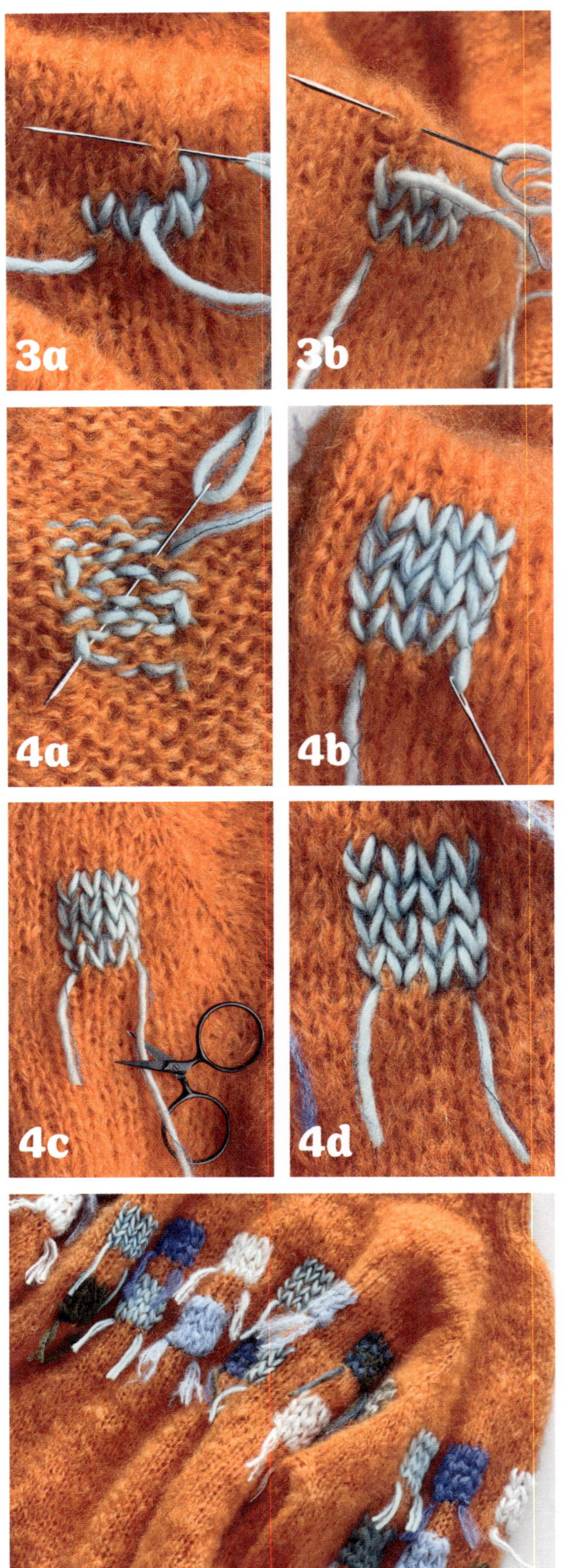

1. Start by placing stitch markers over the knitting, each representing a square. Remember, there are two rows of squares across the whole knitted area. To mark, first find the centre front of the area to be embroidered then place a stitch marker there – this will be the middle of the first square. Count two knit stitches either side of the marker; these will be covered in duplicate stitch. Count four knit stitches to the left of the left-hand duplicate stitches; this is the gap between the squares. Count two more knit stitches to the left then add a stitch marker – this is the second square. Repeat all across the whole knitting. You want complete squares, not half squares, so if you can't add any more whole squares that's fine. Note that the number of squares in the row will vary, depending on your own knitted piece.

Note: If you are embroidering a garment, I recommend trying it on before stitching, to check that you are happy with the positioning of the marked squares.

2. Row 1: Once you're happy with the marked stitches, you can start to embroider from left to right or right to left, whichever feels more natural to you. You'll be starting with the bottom-left or bottom-right stitch of the square design, then embroider row by row upwards. From the right side of the knitting, take the threaded needle down at the bottom of the 'V' of the knit stitch two stitches below the one you wish to cover, then bring it out at the base of the intended knit stitch to embroider. Pull through, leaving a 5cm / 2in end hanging for a fringe. Embroider a row of four duplicate stitches as described on page 16 – I worked each duplicate stitch over two knit stitches in height, but with your own project you may prefer to work over just one stitch in height.

3. Make three more rows of four duplicate stitches, above the first row.

4. After working the last stitch, weave the needle diagonally through the back of the stitches on the wrong side of the work (**4a**); this secures the thread. Then, bring the needle through to the right side in the corner opposite to where you began (**4b**), and cut the end to approx. 5cm / 2in, making a mirrored fringe (**4c**). One square complete (**4d**).

5. Using your stitch markers to help you, repeat steps 2–4 until you have embroidered the whole first row of squares.

6. Row 2: Following the same process for row 1, described in steps 2–5, embroider another row of squares below the first one, five stitches down. The embroidery is complete.

Have It All

These large, textured, sunflower-style flowers give a fun, retro feel to any knitted item. The flowers are embroidered with just three colours and three embroidery stitches in a random fashion across the knitting. I've used three different weights of yarn in the sample opposite, to add subtle changes in texture, but you could use just two for your own embroidery work.

Embroidery techniques

- Lazy daisy (detached chain) stitch
- Chain stitch
- Backstitch

Notions

- Two long, thin, sharp yarn needles – one for thin yarn and one for thick
- Scissors
- Stitch markers
- Embroidery frame (optional)

Yarn

Sandnes Garn: Kos
(62% alpaca, 29% nylon, 9% wool; chunky /bulky / weight 5; 50g / 150m / 164yd)

50g Natural 1012 (off-white)

Sandnes Garn: PetiteKnit Double Sunday (100% merino; DK / light worsted / weight 3; 50g / 108m / 118yd)

50g Statement Green 8236 (bright green)

Sandnes Garn: Tynn Silk Mohair
(57% mohair, 28% silk, 15% wool; 2-ply / lace / weight 0; 25g / 212m / 232yd)

25g Light Copper Brown 3535 (rust)

INSTRUCTIONS

Read through all the instructions before you start to embroider.

The flower head is made up of three parts: two rings of chain stitch, three rounds of lazy daisy (detached chain) stitch, and one ring of backstitch between the lazy-daisy petals and chain-stitch centre. A backstitched green stalk with two chain-stitched leaves finishes off each retro flower.

Place stitch markers on the knitting where you want the flowers, ensuring there's a nice even spread of flowers across the whole knitted piece. (Or, if you'd prefer fewer flowers, just have three across the front as in the left-hand sweater below.) If you find it helpful, you can draw guide lines for the rings of chain stitch and backstitch, as I did for the sample opposite. The innermost chain-stitch ring is approx. 4–5cm / 1½–2in in diameter.

If you're embroidering a garment, I recommend trying it on before stitching, to ensure you're happy with the overall arrangement of flowers.

EMBROIDERY MOTIF

(shown at actual size)

1. Centre: Start by embroidering the innermost chain-stitch ring with two strands of Tynn Silk Mohair in Light Copper Brown. The stitches should be approx. 1cm / ½in long. Embroider a second ring inside the first one. Take care not to pull the yarn too tight.

2. Petals – round 1: Change to a single strand of Kos in Natural. Embroider a round of lazy daisy (detached chain) stitches outside the rings of chain stitches. For my sample, I embroidered roughly 22 lazy daisy (detached chain) stitches. Start each stitch by bringing the needle up from the wrong side at the edge of the chain stitches.

3. Petals – round 2: For the next round of petals, work each lazy daisy (detached chain) stitch above and in between two lazy daisy (detached chain) stitches from round 1.

4. Petals – round 3: For the third and final round of petals, work each lazy daisy (detached chain) stitch above and in between two lazy daisy (detached chain) stitches from round 2, but this time leaving a gap of two lazy daisy (detached chain) stitches from round 2 between each of these new stitches.

5. Outline: Change to two strands of PetiteKnit Double Sunday in Statement Green. Embroider a ring of backstitch between the outer ring of chain stitches in the centre of the flower and round 1 of lazy daisy (detached chain) stitches.

6. Stalk: With two strands of PetiteKnit Double Sunday in Statement Green, embroider a stalk measuring approx. 9cm / 3½in long using backstitch.

7. Leaves: About halfway up the stalk, embroider two leaves in chain stitch using two strands PetiteKnit Double Sunday in Statement Green. For each leaf, start by stitching a central line of chain stitch (the stem) approx. 4cm / 1½in long. Then, either side of the central line, embroider two curving rows of backstitch for the leaves – refer to the diagram opposite for guidance.

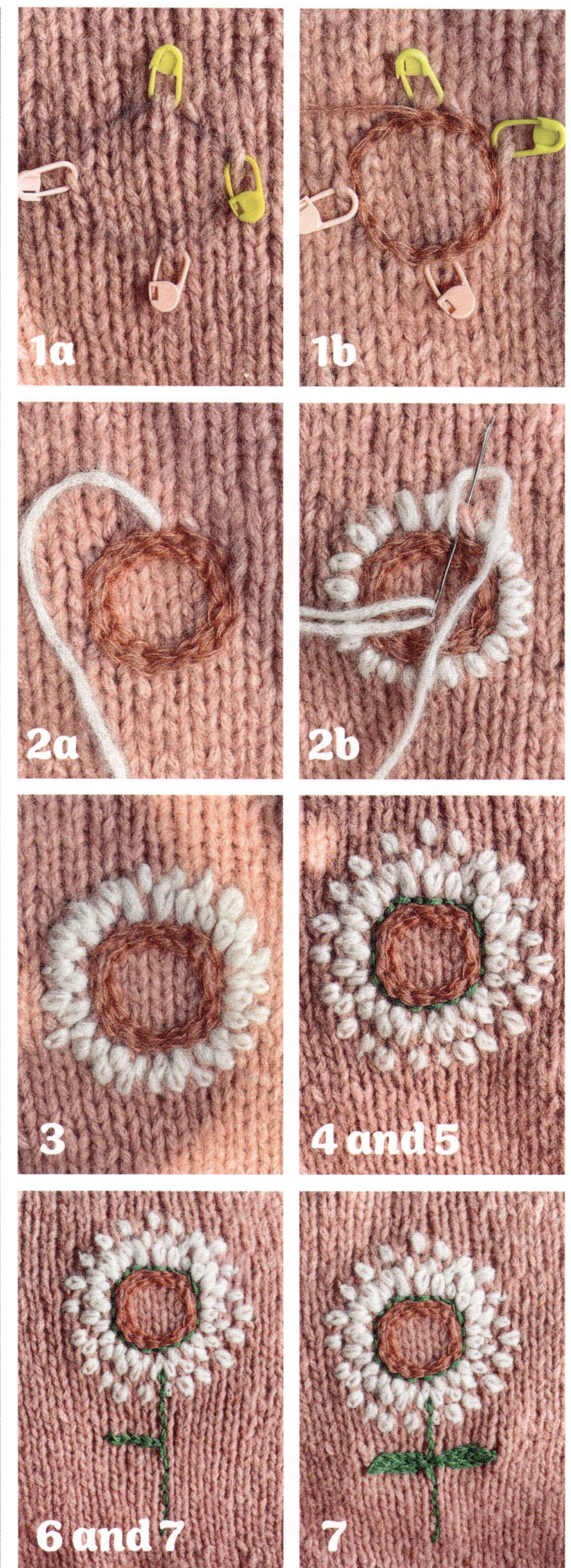

ACKNOWLEDGEMENTS

First of all, I have to thank Liv Loftesnes. Many thanks for getting in touch and making me believe that I could write this book.

Thank you to my gifted test knitters:
Maria Schei Mogenstad
Thea Skåra Loug
Torbjørg Randa
Malin Therese Olsen
Marita Gravdal
Anna Johansson

A big thank you to the hardworking models who hung in there and gave their all – you were absolutely brilliant:
Anna Loug Grastveit
Adrian Egeland
Thea Skåra Loug
Eirik Handeland
Line Pettersen
Emilie Løining Røe

Thank you so much to Truls Skåra Loug for all the help with the computer every time I got stuck, and to Anna and Adrian for all the trips you made to Cappelen Damm with knitted garments for me.

Many thanks to Siv Teigen for lending us your seaside cabin; it provided us with a great base during shoot days.

Many thanks to our photographer, Nettan Dahlqvist; your warm, inviting personality helped to create some magical and memorable days in Egersund.

Many thanks to the amazing Ingrid Wærp (editor), Kamilla Ildahl Berg (designer) and Kaja Kvernbakken (proofreader and specialist consultant) for being so patient, and giving me the time I needed to write the manuscript. Ingrid, you are always so positive, supportive, understanding and solution-oriented. I really appreciate that. Kamilla, many thanks for the great job you've done; your keen eye for detail and colour has left its mark on the book. Kaja, you are a brilliant proofreader. I have learnt a lot from you that I will take with me in future. I can't thank you enough!

First published in the UK in 2026 by
Search Press Limited
Wellwood, North Farm Road,
Tunbridge Wells, Kent TN2 3DR

1 2 3 4 5 6 7 8 9 10

Originally published in Oslo, Norway as *Broderi på strikk* in 2023
by CAPPELEN DAMM AS

English translation from the original Norwegian by Tankerton Translations.

Original cover design: Kamilla Ildahl Berg
Photography: Nettan Dahlqvist and Diana Loug
Reproduction photography: Narayana Press
Styling: Nettan Dahlqvist and Diana Loug
Illustrations: Narayana Press and Diana Loug
Typesetting: Kamilla Ildahl Berg

ISBN: 978-1-80092-340-9
ebook ISBN: 978-1-80093-327-9

BOOKMARKED HUB
For further ideas and inspiration, and to join our free online community, visit www.bookmarkedhub.com

PUBLISHERS' NOTES
Metric measurements are used in this book; the imperial conversions are rounded to the nearest ¼in, ¼yd or ¼oz. Always use either metric or imperial measurements, not a combination of both.

Search Press Limited, CAPPELEN DAMM AS and the author can accept no responsibility for any consequences arising from the information, advice or instructions given in this publication.

For errata, please visit our website (www.searchpress.com) or the Bookmarked Hub (www.bookmarkedhub.com).

GPSR information can be found at www.searchpress.com

Printed in China, TT102025

ABOUT THE AUTHOR
You are invited to visit Diana Loug's social media pages:
– Instagram, via @gollestrikk
– Pinterest profile, via @gollestrikk

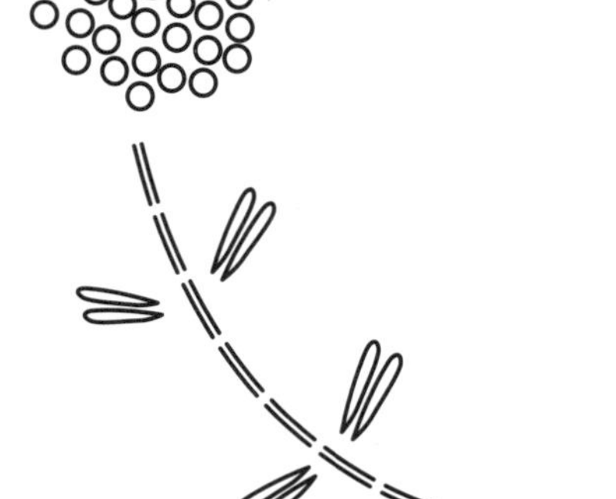